GREAT **HEALTHY** FOOD™
FOR
STRONG BONES

FIONA HUNTER & EMMA-LEE GOW

CARROLL & BROWN PUBLISHERS LIMITED

First published in 2002 in the United
Kingdom by:

Carroll & Brown Publishers Limited
20 Lonsdale Road
Queen's Park
London NW6 6RD

Managing Editor Becky Alexander
Editor Jessica Hughes
Designer Justin Ford
Photography David Murray
Food Stylist Clare Lewis
**Consultant for National Osteoporosis
 Society** Dr Sue New

Copyright © 2002
Carroll & Brown Limited

A CIP catalogue record for this book is
available from the British Library.
ISBN 1-903258-32-4

Reproduced by Colourscan, Singapore
Printed and bound in Great Britain by
The Bath Press
First edition

The moral right of Fiona Hunter and
Emma-Lee Gow to be identified as the
authors of this work has been asserted in
accordance with the Copyright, Designs
and Patents Act of 1988.

Contents

INTRODUCTION   4

1 Start the Day   10

2 Soups & Appetizers   20

3 Light Snacks & Lunches   32

4 Main Courses   46

5 On the Side   90

6 Puddings & Treats   100

7 Home Bakes   112

RECIPE LIST AND
NUTRITIONAL ANALYSIS   124

INDEX   127

Introduction

One of the most important ways in which we can develop and maintain strong bones is through a healthy diet; choosing a healthy, well balanced and varied diet that includes foods from each of the main food groups will help ensure a good intake of vitamins and minerals, especially calcium, which is essential for good bone health. Building strong bones when we are young and helping to reduce the effects of bone-density loss as we get older means that we can alleviate many of the symptoms of osteoporosis. This book features a wide variety of delicious recipes that have been devised to help you develop a diet that is great for strong, healthy bones and that will appeal to all the family. The recipes will also fit easily into your lifestyle, as the dishes are easy to prepare and all the ingredients are readily available in supermarkets.

Diet and Osteoporosis

A poor diet will increase the risk of osteoporosis (also known as brittle bone disease) later in life. Osteoporosis affects 1 in 3 women and 1 in 12 men during their lifetimes. Bones are made up of a thick outer shell with a strong, dense inner mesh that has a honeycomb-like structure. A good calcium intake is vital because this gives the bones their strength and rigidity. As bone becomes old it is removed by the body and replaced with new bone – it has been calculated that adults replace their entire skeletons every 7 to 10 years. Calcium, therefore, gets deposited and withdrawn from the skeleton on a daily basis. As we get older, this renewal process slows down and bone-density loss increases. When this happens, the holes in the bone's inner mesh gradually become bigger and the bones become more fragile and, therefore, more likely to fracture or break – this is known as osteoporosis. However, by maximising bone mass early in life and by maintaining a healthy diet, we can reduce the effects of this process.

CALCIUM FOR EVERYONE

It's never too early or too late to begin eating for strong bones. A good calcium intake during childhood, adolescence and early adulthood, while the bones are still growing, will help to protect your bones throughout life. By the age of 25, your bones have reached their maximum potential strength, so it is important to invest in them in the early years. As we move into later life, maintaining a calcium-rich diet is equally important, in order to reduce the effects of bone loss. Bone density begins to decrease around age 35, so it is essential to maintain a bone-friendly diet throughout life.

Pregnant women need a good calcium intake to provide for the calcium needs of their babies. People on low-fat diets also need to ensure they are not missing out on calcium-rich foods such as dairy products. It is important to remember that low-

THE NATIONAL OSTEOPOROSIS SOCIETY

The NOS is the UK's authoritative voice on osteoporosis and the only national charity dedicated to improving its diagnosis, prevention and treatment. Since 1986, the NOS has worked hard to raise public awareness and to offer support to people with osteoporosis, their families and carers through a range of information booklets, a national telephone helpline and a network of support groups.

The NOS raises awareness of bone health among people of all ages and fundraises for research into osteoporosis, to increase understanding of the disease and improve treatment options and patient care. Many people know what osteoporosis is, but few realise how serious it can be or that they are at personal risk. For more information, visit www.nos.org.uk

RECOMMENDED DAILY INTAKES OF CALCIUM

Age	Daily intake*	Number of servings**
Children, 4–6 years	450 mg	2
Children, 7–10 years	550 mg	2–3
Boys, 11–18 years	1000 mg	3–4
Girls, 11–18 years	800 mg	2–3
Men and women, 19–50 years	700 mg	2–3
Men and women, 50 years and over	700 mg	2–3
Pregnant women	700 mg	2–3
Breastfeeding women	700 + 550 mg	4–5

* Recommended figures from National Osteoporosis Society

** 1 serving = 1 glass of milk, 150 g yogurt or 40 g hard full-fat cheese.

A HEALTHY LIFESTYLE

As well as a bone-friendly diet, there are other ways in which we can improve bone strength. Weight-bearing exercise, for example walking, jogging, tennis or aerobics, improves bone density, and balance exercises, such as yoga, reduce the risk of falling – active people have 20–45 per cent less risk of fracture. Exercise such as swimming and cycling is good for overall fitness, but is of no benefit to the bones. Also, giving up smoking is vital for strong bones, because it damages the cells that make new bone.

fat dairy products can still be a good source of calcium, because when fat is removed to make reduced or low-fat products, the calcium remains (in fact, pint for pint, skimmed milk contains slightly more calcium than whole milk). This is especially important for teenage girls, who are more likely to embark on low-fat diets at a time when good calcium intake is vital.

BONE-FRIENDLY FOODS

As part of a diet for strong bones, and for your health in general, you need to eat a healthy, well balanced and varied diet that includes at least 5 servings of fruit and/or vegetables a day, plenty of wholegrain cereals and not too much sugar or fat. The following vitamins and minerals are particularly good for strong bones.

Calcium This is the most vital mineral for strong bones. Calcium is also essential for blood clotting, muscle contraction and nerve function and, if we don't take in enough, the body uses the calcium in the bones to supply the muscles, heart and nerves. In the average British diet, milk and other dairy products provide over 50 per cent of dietary calcium, but it is also found in beans and pulses, canned fish that is eaten along with its bones, for example salmon, pilchards and sardines, some green vegetables, such as spinach and broccoli, and nuts and fruit.

Vitamin D This is vital for the absorption of calcium and is produced when the skin is exposed to sunlight. About 15–20 minutes of sunlight a day on the face and arms during the summer months enables the body to store enough vitamin D to last the rest of the year. Most people obtain sufficient vitamin D in this way but some groups, such as the elderly, housebound or people who wear clothes that cover most of their bodies, may have insufficient vitamin D. Good food sources of vitamin D are oil-rich fish, egg yolks, liver and margarine.

Magnesium Recent studies suggest that magnesium has an important role in helping to keep our bones healthy. Good sources of magnesium include Brazil nuts, sesame seeds, bananas, pine nuts, cashew nuts and dark green leafy vegetables, such as spinach and watercress.

Vitamin K Studies have found that women who have a good intake of vitamin K have denser bones. Foods rich in vitamin K include curly kale, broccoli and spinach.

Fruit and vegetables There is growing evidence suggesting a positive link between eating plenty of fruit and vegetables and better bone density. Aim to eat at least five portions of fruit or vegetables a day.

BE CAREFUL WITH . . .
Protein High intakes of protein increase the excretion of calcium in the urine. For most people, however, protein intakes are not high enough to give cause for concern, but it could be a problem if you take protein supplements or follow a high-protein, weight-reducing diet.

Salt High sodium (salt) intake can also increase the loss of calcium in the urine. Over three-quarters of the sodium in our diet comes from processed foods, so the simplest way to reduce sodium intake is to eat fewer processed foods. Food with less salt may initially taste bland, but by gradually reducing the amount of salt you eat, the tastebuds will adapt as the salt receptors on the tongue become more sensitive. Try using other flavourings such as herbs and spices, lemon or mustard.

Caffeine High intakes of caffeine can reduce absorption of calcium – each cup of coffee prevents the absorption of 6 mg of calcium, which is the amount you would get from 1 teaspoon of milk. The effect of caffeine is relatively small, but people with very high intakes should cut back.

Alcohol Excessive intakes of alcohol can damage the cells that make new bone. If you drink, stay within the recommended guidelines (no more than 2–3 units of alcohol a day for women or 3–4 units for men).

Fizzy drinks Phosphate, in the form of phosphoric acid, is used as a preservative in most canned fizzy drinks. When phosphorus levels exceed calcium levels in the blood, the body responds by stimulating bone breakdown to release calcium into the blood. Although there is no hard scientific evidence to show a detrimental effect on bone health, it is probably wise to cut back if you have an excessive intake, and to limit the amount of fizzy drinks your children consume. Instead, why not offer a glass of cold milk?

NOTES TO THE COOK
To minimise the fat content of the dishes, all milk should be semi-skimmed, unless specified in the ingredients. Also, because a high sodium intake is not good for your bones, or your general health, the sodium content of the recipes has been kept as low as possible. If you do add salt, keep it to a minimum.

1

Start the Day

Whether you prefer a sweet or savoury breakfast, this chapter offers a variety of calcium-rich recipes that will give you the best possible start to the day.

SWEET FRUIT PORRIDGE

125 g raisins or chopped dried dates

150 ml water

150 ml milk

125 g rolled oats

Pinch of salt

Serves 4

Extra sweetness is released from the dried fruit when it is liquidised, so you don't need to add any sugar or honey.

1 In a blender or food processor, blend the raisins or chopped dates with the water and milk until smooth.

2 In a heavy based saucepan, combine the fruit mixture with the oats and add a pinch of salt. Bring to the boil, stirring steadily. Simmer the mixture, uncovered, stirring occasionally, for 4–5 minutes until the desired consistency is reached. Serve with extra milk, if liked.

APPLE & BLUEBERRY MUESLI

5 tablespoons rolled oats

2 tablespoons sultanas

2 tablespoons flaked almonds

8 tablespoons apple juice

250 ml plain bio-yogurt

200 ml semi-skimmed milk

1 tablespoon clear honey

2 crisp eating apples, cored and grated

75 g fresh blueberries

Serves 2–3

This muesli mix is packed full of delicious ingredients that are good for your bone health, and with none of the additives found in some commercially produced cereals. Soaking the oats in apple juice and milk gives this a fruity flavour, while keeping the calcium content high.

1 Mix together the oats, sultanas, almonds and apple juice and allow to stand for a few minutes, until the juice is absorbed.

2 Stir the yogurt, milk, honey and grated apple into the oats and leave to stand for 15 minutes.

3 Stir in the blueberries and serve.

SPICED FRUIT COMPOTE

Dried fruits are useful source of calcium, particularly for people on dairy-free diets. They also make a tasty snack in between meals. This compote can also be served with natural yogurt as a dessert.

1   Put the dried fruit, cinnamon stick and cardamon pods in a large bowl. Pour over the apple and mango juice and 450 ml of boiling water. Allow to cool, cover and leave overnight in the fridge.

2   Remove the cardamon pods and cinnamon stick. Mix the cornflour with enough cold water to make a smooth paste. Drain the liquid from the fruit and place in a small saucepan. Stir in the cornflour paste and bring to the boil. Cook for 1 minute, or until thickened, then pour over the compote. Set aside and leave to cool.

3   Place 2 Scotch pancakes on each of 4 plates with a large spoonful of the fruit compote and a large spoonful of Greek yogurt. Sprinkle with orange zest to serve.

250 g mixed ready-to-eat dried fruit, such as apricots, apples and prunes or papaya, mango and pineapple

1 stick cinnamon

3 whole green cardamom pods, lightly crushed

225 ml apple juice

225 ml mango juice

2 teaspoons cornflour

TO SERVE

8 ready-made Scotch pancakes

4 tablespoons Greek yogurt

Zest of 1 orange

Serves 4

DRIED FRUIT SPREAD

175 g ready-to-eat dried apricots, roughly chopped

175 g dried figs, roughly chopped

75 g ready-to-eat dried apple, roughly chopped

Zest of 1 orange

200 ml unsweetened orange juice

Makes 450 g (about 25 portions)

This is a healthier alternative to jam or marmalade and is delicious spread on warm, buttered toast. You could also try stirring a tablespoon of the spread into low-fat plain yogurt. It will keep for 3 weeks if stored in jars in the fridge.

1 Place the apricots, figs, apple, orange zest and juice into a pan and bring to the boil. Reduce the heat and simmer for 20–30 minutes, or until the mixture is thick and the orange juice has evaporated. You can add a little more orange juice if necessary, but the final purée should be quite thick.

2 Transfer the mixture to a blender and purée until smooth. Spoon the purée into jars and store in the fridge.

BAGELS WITH RASPBERRIES & RICOTTA

100 g fresh raspberries

75 g ricotta cheese

1 tablespoon icing sugar

2 cinnamon or fruit bagels, halved

Serves 2

Ricotta cheese contains a lot less fat than most other creamy cheeses, but still provides useful amounts of calcium.

1 Place the raspberries, ricotta and icing sugar in a bowl and mash until combined. Place in the fridge until needed.

2 Lightly toast the bagels and spread over the raspberry and ricotta mixture.

BANANA & ALMOND SMOOTHIE

2 ripe bananas

450 ml semi-skimmed milk

40 g ground almonds

1–2 teaspoons honey, to sweeten (optional)

Serves 2

The combination of milk and fruit in smoothies is great for strong bones. Almonds are an excellent source of vitamin E, along with the minerals calcium, magnesium, phosphorus and copper. They also give this smoothie a rich, creamy taste.

1 Peel and slice the bananas, place in a freezer-proof container and freeze for at least 2 hours, or overnight.

2 Place the bananas, milk, almonds and honey in a blender or food processor and blend until thick and frothy. Pour into glasses and serve immediately.

APRICOT & ORANGE SMOOTHIE

Both dried apricots and orange juice are useful sources of calcium, making this a good alternative to milk-based smoothies for people on dairy-free diets.

1   Place the apricots in a small saucepan and pour over 300 ml water. Bring to the boil and simmer over a low heat for 10 minutes, or until the apricots are soft.

2   Place the apricots and any remaining water in a liquidiser. Pour in the orange juice and purée until smooth.

3   To serve, pour into glasses and add a couple of ice cubes to serve.

125 g ready-to-eat dried apricots, chopped into small pieces

400 ml orange juice

Serves 2

STRAWBERRY SMOOTHIE

Strawberries are rich in vitamin C, which is needed for healthy bones. The fortified soya milk is a good non-dairy alternative to cow's milk and also adds vital calcium.

1   Switch the freezer to 'fast freeze'. Roughly chop the strawberries and place in a plastic freezerproof container. Freeze for at least 2 hours, or preferably overnight. If your freezer does not have a 'fast freeze' function, you will need to freeze the strawberries overnight.

2   Remove the strawberry pieces from the freezer and turn the freezer setting back to 'normal', if necessary. Reserve about 200 g of the strawberry pieces to decorate, then purée the remainder in a food processor or blender with the soya milk until smooth.

3   Pour the smoothie into 4 large glasses and decorate with the remaining strawberries. Garnish with mint sprigs to serve.

750 g fresh ripe strawberries

600 ml sweetened calcium-fortified soya milk

Fresh mint sprigs, to garnish

Serves 4

CHEESY SCRAMBLED EGGS

This breakfast provides a perfect combination of ingredients for strong bones – cheese is rich in calcium while the eggs provide vitamin D, which is essential for optimum calcium absorption.

1 Mix the eggs and milk together and season to taste. Heat the butter in a non-stick saucepan. Add the eggs and cook over a low heat, stirring continuously.

2 Once the eggs are scrambled, remove from the heat and stir in the cheese and spring onions. Serve immediately on wholemeal toast.

4 eggs, beaten

2 tablespoons semi-skimmed milk

Salt and pepper, to taste

1 teaspoon butter

50 g Cheddar cheese, grated

4 spring onions, finely chopped

Wholemeal toast, to serve

Serves 2

SMOKED HADDOCK OMELETTE

This omelette is a substantial, nutritious breakfast that is still quick and easy to make.

1 Place the fish in a shallow pan and cover with water. Bring to the boil, reduce the heat and simmer gently for 5 minutes, or until the fish is cooked. Drain, then flake the fish, discarding the skin and bones.

2 Preheat the grill. Beat the egg yolks in a bowl with the milk and seasoning. Stir in the flaked fish. Whisk the egg whites until stiff then, using a metal spoon, fold into the yolk mixture.

3 Heat the butter in an omelette pan. Pour in the egg mixture and cook for 2–3 minutes or until the bottom of the omelette is set. Slide the omelette onto a flameproof serving dish.

4 Sprinkle over the cheese and place under the grill for 2–3 minutes, or until the top has set and the cheese melted. Garnish with chives to serve.

125 g smoked haddock

4 eggs, separated

2 tablespoons full-fat milk

Salt and pepper, to taste

15 g butter

40 g Gruyère cheese, grated

Fresh chives, chopped, to garnish

Serves 2

SOFT EGGS WITH SOURED CREAM & SMOKED SALMON

This is a special treat for breakfast or brunch, or a tasty and nutritious snack at any time. Both eggs and smoked salmon provide useful amounts of vitamin D, which helps the absorption of calcium. However, if you are serving this dish to anyone elderly, a pregnant woman, young children or people who have immune deficiency disease, boil the eggs for slightly longer, to make sure that they are well-cooked. This will eliminate any risk of salmonella.

4 eggs

100 g smoked salmon

200 ml soured cream

1 teaspoon black peppercorns

2 punnets mustard and cress, to garnish

4 slices Granary toast, buttered, to serve

Serves 4

1 Lower the eggs into a pan of simmering water, making sure that the water covers them completely. Cook for 3½–5 minutes until soft-boiled. Drain and rinse under cool running water, until the eggs are cool enough to handle, then shell.

2 Meanwhile, chop roughly the smoked salmon and stir into the soured cream. Crack the black peppercorns, using a pestle and mortar. If you don't have a pestle and mortar, grind the peppercorns as coarsely as you can.

3 Halve the eggs and arrange on individual serving plates. Spoon over the smoked salmon and soured cream mixture. Scatter with the cracked black peppercorns and garnish with mustard and cress. Serve with buttered Granary toast.

SMOKED HADDOCK & SWEETCORN FRITTERS

Serve these light and tasty fritters with grilled tomatoes for a balanced and nutritious start to the day.

1 Place the haddock in a shallow pan and pour over the milk. Bring to the boil, then cover and simmer for 6–7 minutes, or until the fish is cooked. Remove the fish from the milk, discard the skin and bones and flake the fish. Strain the milk and reserve.

2 Place the flour in a large bowl and make a well in the centre. Whisk in the egg yolk and enough of the reserved milk to make a thick batter (you should need about 125 ml). Stir in the sweetcorn and haddock and season to taste. In a clean bowl, whisk the egg white until it forms soft peaks, then carefully fold into the batter.

3 Cook the mixture in batches by dropping spoonfuls onto a lightly greased griddle or heavy based frying pan. Cook for 2–3 minutes, then turn carefully and cook for a further 2–3 minutes, until golden brown. Serve with the grilled tomatoes.

200 g smoked haddock

175 ml semi-skimmed milk

100 g plain flour

1 egg, separated

125 g canned sweetcorn, drained

Salt and pepper, to taste

Vegetable oil, for frying

6 grilled tomatoes, halved, to serve

Serves 4 (makes 8 fritters)

STUFFED PORTOBELLO MUSHROOMS

Mushrooms are often part of breakfast dishes, and this recipe uses them in a creative and interesting way. This is a tasty and satisfying breakfast or brunch that takes just a few minutes to prepare. Serve with buttered Granary toast.

1 Preheat the oven to 220°C, gas mark 7. Wipe the mushrooms with a damp cloth, then remove and finely chop the stalks. Lightly brush the cap of each mushroom with a little olive oil and place on a baking sheet.

2 Heat the remaining oil in a large non-stick frying pan and add the chopped mushroom stalks, onions and celery. Cook over a medium heat, stirring occasionally, for 3–4 minutes, or until the vegetables are beginning to soften.

3 Stir in the breadcrumbs, ham, parsley and lemon zest, then season with salt and pepper.

4 Spoon the breadcrumb mixture into the mushrooms then sprinkle with the Parmesan cheese. Bake in the oven for 15–20 minutes, or until the mushrooms are tender and golden. Garnish with sprigs of flat-leaf parsley.

8 Portobello (large flat) mushrooms

2 tablespoons olive oil

1 medium red onion, finely chopped

6 sticks celery, finely chopped

150 g fine white breadcrumbs

225 g wafer-thin smoked ham, roughly chopped

6 tablespoons fresh flat-leaf parsley, chopped

Zest of 1 large lemon

Salt and pepper, to taste

3 tablespoons Parmesan cheese, freshly grated

Sprigs of flat-leaf parsley, to garnish

Serves 4

2
Soups & Starters

THE DISHES IN THIS CHAPTER MAKE
THE MOST OF BOTH DAIRY AND NON-
DAIRY SOURCES OF CALCIUM AND
OTHER VITAMINS AND MINERALS. MANY
OF THE RECIPES CAN BE PREPARED IN
ADVANCE AND SERVED WHEN
REQUIRED.

BROCCOLI & STILTON SOUP

Broccoli is an excellent source of calcium and vitamin C, so is ideal as part of a bone-friendly diet. Serve this soup with crusty bread.

I tablespoon vegetable oil

I medium onion, finely chopped

I clove garlic, peeled and finely chopped

I large floury potato, such as Maris Piper, peeled and finely diced

600 ml vegetable stock

450 g broccoli, trimmed and roughly chopped

300 ml semi-skimmed milk

Salt and pepper, to taste

125 g Stilton, crumbled

Serves 4–6

1 Heat the oil in large pan, then add the onion and garlic and cook for 3–4 minutes. Add the potato and continue to cook, stirring occasionally, for 2–3 minutes.

2 Add the stock and bring to the boil, then reduce the heat, cover and cook for 10 minutes. Add the broccoli and simmer for 5–10 minutes, or until the broccoli is just tender.

3 Place the mixture in a blender and purée until smooth, then return to the pan. Stir in the milk, season to taste and gently reheat. When the soup is hot, stir in the Stilton and, once the cheese has melted into the soup, serve.

MOROCCAN SPICED CHICKPEA SOUP

This wholesome soup is the perfect way to keep warm on a cold day. Chickpeas, along with other beans and pulses, are a useful source of calcium, particularly for people who don't eat dairy products.

2 tablespoons olive oil

I large onion, chopped

I clove garlic, peeled and finely chopped

2 medium carrots, thickly sliced

2 sticks celery, thickly sliced

2 courgettes, thickly sliced

2 teaspoons ground cumin

I teaspoon turmeric

I tablespoon tomato purée

400 g can chopped tomatoes

400 g can chickpeas, drained

600 ml vegetable stock

3 tablespoons fresh coriander, chopped, to garnish

Serves 4

1 Heat the oil in a large non-stick pan and cook the onion and garlic for 5 minutes until soft.

2 Add the carrots, celery and courgettes and cook for a further 4–5 minutes, stirring occasionally.

3 Add the cumin and turmeric and stir to coat the vegetables. Add the tomato purée, canned tomatoes, chickpeas and stock. Bring to the boil then cover and simmer for 20–30 minutes, until the vegetables are soft. Garnish with fresh coriander and serve.

ROASTED PEPPER SOUP WITH FETA & BASIL

The roasted peppers give a subtle sweet flavour to this soup which is enhanced by the feta and basil. To save time, you could substitute cans or jars of roasted peppers or sweet pimentos.

1 Preheat the oven to 200°C, gas mark 6. Put the pepper halves cut-side down on a large baking sheet and roast for 25–30 minutes or until the skins are blackened. Leave to cool slightly then put the peppers into a polythene bag for 10 minutes, until the skins loosen. Remove the skins, chop the flesh roughly and set aside.

2 Heat the oil in large saucepan and cook the onion and garlic for 5 minutes, until soft. Add the chopped peppers, tomatoes, vegetable stock and seasoning. Bring to the boil, cover and simmer for 20 minutes. Remove from the heat and purée the soup in a blender or processor (you will probably need to do this in batches). Return to the pan, add the shredded basil and reheat.

3 To serve, spoon into soup bowls and scatter over the feta. Garnish with basil leaves and a grinding of black pepper.

4 large red peppers, halved, cored and deseeded or 450 g jar roasted red peppers, drained and rinsed

2 tablespoons olive oil

1 large red onion, roughly chopped

2 cloves garlic, peeled and roughly chopped

400 g can chopped tomatoes

900 ml vegetable stock

Salt and pepper, to taste

2 tablespoons fresh basil, shredded

100 g feta cheese, crumbled

Fresh basil leaves, to garnish

Serves 6

FRENCH ONION SOUP

Here, this traditional soup is served ladled over toasted bread with a sprinkling of Gruyère cheese. For a change, the Gruyère can be replaced with goat's cheese, Emmenthal, mozzarella or any blue cheese.

1 Melt the butter in a large saucepan, add the onions and cook gently for 15–20 minutes until they are golden brown.

2 Sift the flour into the pan and cook, stirring continuously, for 1 minute. Stir in the stock, seasoning and add the bay leaf. Bring to the boil, cover and simmer for 30 minutes.

3 Cut the French loaf diagonally into 1 cm slices. Heat the grill to medium and toast the bread lightly on both sides. Place two slices in each of 4 ovenproof soup bowls and ladle over the hot soup, discarding the bay leaf.

4 Turn the grill to high. Sprinkle the Gruyère cheese over the soup and place under the grill until the cheese is melted and bubbling. Serve immediately.

50 g butter

3 large onions, thinly sliced

1 tablespoon plain flour

900 ml vegetable stock

Salt and pepper, to taste

1 bay leaf

½ medium French loaf

75 g Gruyère cheese, grated

Serves 4

GARDEN PEA & WATERCRESS SOUP WITH SESAME CROUTONS

The bright colour of this creamy, fresh-tasting soup makes it an eye-catching starter, while the sesame croutons add texture.

1 To make the croutons, brush the ciabatta pieces with 2 tablespoons of the oil and sprinkle with the sesame seeds. Heat the remaining oil in a non-stick pan and cook the croutons over a high heat for 3–4 minutes until crisp and golden. Remove and drain on kitchen paper, then set aside to cool.

2 To make the soup, melt the butter in a large saucepan. Add the onion and cook for 5 minutes until soft, then add the peas, watercress, stock and seasoning. Bring slowly to the boil, lower the heat, cover and simmer for 5 minutes.

3 Allow the soup to cool slightly, then process in a blender or food processor until smooth (you will probably need to do this in batches). Pour into a clean saucepan, season to taste and reheat.

4 Drizzle with crème fraîche and garnish with chopped mint and the sesame croutons. Serve with chunks of wholemeal or granary bread.

FOR THE SESAME CROUTONS

3 slices ciabatta bread, cut into small pieces

3 tablespoons olive oil

1 tablespoon sesame seeds

FOR THE SOUP

40 g butter

1 large onion, finely chopped

450 g fresh or frozen peas

75 g fresh watercress, roughly chopped

1 litre hot vegetable stock

Salt and pepper, to taste

4–6 tablespoons crème fraîche, to garnish

Fresh mint leaves, to garnish

Serves 4–6

SMOKED HADDOCK & SWEETCORN CHOWDER

Using semi-skimmed milk gives this soup a creamy rich taste, while reducing the fat content of the dish. It is also a good source of calcium. The soup is delicious served with crusty bread.

25 g butter

1 medium onion, peeled and finely chopped

2 medium floury potatoes, such as Maris Piper, peeled and cut into small cubes

400 ml fish stock

300 g canned sweetcorn, drained

400 ml semi-skimmed milk

450 g skinless smoked haddock fillets, cut into bite-sized pieces

Salt and pepper, to taste

Fresh parsley, chopped, to garnish

Serves 4

1 Melt the butter in a large saucepan, add the onion and cook over a gentle heat for 5 minutes until soft. Add the potato and continue cooking for a further 2 minutes.

2 Add the fish stock and bring to the boil. Reduce the heat, cover and simmer for about 10–15 minutes, or until the potatoes are tender. Roughly mash the potatoes.

3 Add the sweetcorn and milk and return to the boil. Reduce the heat and simmer for 5 minutes. Stir in the fish and continue to cook for a further 5 minutes. Season to taste and garnish with chopped parsley.

BAKED RICOTTA WITH ROASTED VINE TOMATOES

This dish is ideal as a starter or a light lunch with a green salad. Mixing Parmesan cheese with the ricotta cheese boosts the flavour as well as the calcium content.

Butter, for greasing

300 g ricotta cheese

125 g Parmesan cheese, freshly grated

2 eggs, separated

Salt and pepper, to taste

4 plum tomatoes, halved

1 tablespoon olive oil

1 tablespoon balsamic vinegar

Serves 4

1 Preheat the oven to 180°C, gas mark 4. Grease a shallow ovenproof dish.

2 Place the ricotta and Parmesan cheeses in a bowl and beat in the egg yolks until the mixture is smooth. Season to taste.

3 In a clean bowl, beat the egg whites until stiff. Using a metal spoon, fold the egg whites into the cheese mixture.

4 Spoon the mixture into the prepared dish and bake for 30–40 minutes, or until slightly risen, golden and firm to the touch. Allow to cool.

5 Place the tomatoes cut-side up on a baking tray. Mix the olive oil and balsamic vinegar together and drizzle over the tomatoes. Season and bake for 20 minutes, or until the tomatoes are softened and slightly charred.

6 Slice the baked cheese into quarters and serve with the tomatoes.

MUSHROOMS & GOAT'S CHEESE IN AUBERGINE PARCELS

These tasty parcels are ideal as a starter, and a rocket salad with balsamic dressing makes a good accompaniment. Mushrooms are rich in copper, which is a vital mineral for strong bones.

1 Cut the aubergine lengthways into thin slices. Sprinkle with salt and set aside for 30 minutes. Rinse well and pat dry with kitchen roll. Brush the aubergine with 1 tablespoon oil and place under a hot grill for 2–3 minutes on each side, until golden brown. Transfer to a plate lined with kitchen paper and set to one side.

2 Heat the remaining oil in large non-stick frying pan, add the garlic, spring onions and mushrooms and cook for 10–15 minutes, until all the liquid has evaporated. Set to one side to cool.

3 Combine the mushroom mixture and the goat's cheese and season to taste. Line the base and sides of two 150 ml ramekin dishes with the grilled aubergine slices, allowing about one third of the slices to hang over the edge. Spoon the mushroom and cheese mixture into the ramekins and fold over the aubergine slices to encase the mixture.

4 Chill for 15 minutes, then turn the parcels out onto a lightly oiled baking sheet. Cook at 190°C, gas mark 5 for 10–15 minutes and serve immediately.

1 long, thin aubergine

Salt, for sprinkling aubergine

2 tablespoons olive oil

1 clove garlic, peeled and finely chopped

4 spring onions, finely chopped

150 g button mushrooms, finely chopped

125 g soft goat's cheese, rind removed

Salt and pepper, to taste

Serves 2

CHERRY TOMATO & GOAT'S CHEESE TARTLETS

These crisp individual pastry cases have a rich cheese and tomato filling and make a great starter. They also make a delicious lunchtime snack, accompanied by a leafy green salad.

1 Preheat the oven to 200°C, gas mark 6. On a lightly floured surface, roll out the puff pastry and use to line four 10 cm tartlet tins. Line the pastry cases with baking parchment and fill with baking beans. Chill for 10 minutes.

2 Bake the pastry cases for 10 minutes. Remove the paper and beans and bake for a further 10 minutes, until the pastry is lightly golden.

3 Meanwhile, heat the oil in a non-stick frying pan. Add the red onion and thyme. Cook gently for 3–4 minutes until soft. Remove from the heat and set aside.

4 Beat the eggs and cream together. Add the Gruyère cheese and cooled onion mixture. Season and mix well. Cut the goat's cheese into 4 round slices. Divide the egg mixture between the tartlets and put 4 cherry tomato halves and 1 goat's cheese slice in each tartlet.

5 Bake the tartlets for 15 minutes until the filling is set. Cool slightly before removing them from the tins. Scatter a few thyme leaves over the warm tartlets just before serving.

Flour, for dusting

225 g ready-made puff pastry

1 tablespoon olive oil

1 medium red onion, finely chopped

1 teaspoon fresh thyme, chopped

2 eggs

150 ml single cream

25 g Gruyère cheese, finely grated

Salt and pepper, to taste

100 g firm, round goat's cheese

8 cherry tomatoes, halved

Few fresh thyme leaves, to garnish

Serves 4

TOMATO & MOZZARELLA SALAD

A classic combination which makes a tasty starter or a welcome accompaniment to most Italian dishes. If you're watching your fat intake, choose reduced-fat mozzarella cheese; although it contains less fat, it is still a good source of calcium. Serve with crusty bread.

1 Whisk together the oil and vinegar to make the dressing. Season to taste.

2 Arrange the tomatoes and mozzarella cheese on a large plate. Drizzle over the dressing and scatter the basil over the top.

6 tablespoons olive oil

2 tablespoons white wine vinegar

Salt and pepper, to taste

3 large beefsteak tomatoes, thickly sliced

2 x 150 g round mozzarella cheeses, thickly sliced

24 leaves fresh basil, roughly torn

Serves 4–6

WATERCRESS, PEAR & ROQUEFORT SALAD

The contrasting flavours in this salad make it an interesting snack, starter or accompaniment. Roquefort, watercress and almonds are all rich in bone-strengthening calcium. Serve with crusty bread.

1 To make the dressing, whisk together the oil, vinegar, mustard and salt.

2 Place the watercress in a large serving bowl. Peel, core and slice the pears and mix into the watercress, along with the cheese and almonds. Drizzle over the dressing and toss.

FOR THE DRESSING

5 tablespoons olive oil

1 tablespoon white wine vinegar

½ teaspoon English mustard powder

Pinch of salt

FOR THE SALAD

150 g watercress, washed

2 ripe pears

200 g Roquefort cheese, crumbled

50 g flaked almonds, lightly toasted

Serves 4

AVOCADO & SMOKED SALMON ROLLS

Reduced-fat soft cheese contains considerably less fat than full-fat cheese, but still contains good amounts of calcium. Oil-rich fish, such as salmon, provide vitamin D which is essential for the absorption of calcium. These rolls are delicious served with wholemeal toast.

1 Remove the flesh of the avocado and mash. Add the cheese, lemon juice and seasoning and mix well. Chill the mixture in the fridge for 15 minutes.

2 Place the strips of salmon on a sheet of greaseproof paper and spread with the avocado mixture. Roll the salmon, from the shortest side, to enclose the avocado. Wrap the salmon rolls in greaseproof paper and place in the fridge until needed – they can prepared up to 4 hours in advance. To serve, garnish with lemon wedges.

1 medium-ripe avocado

125 g reduced-fat soft cheese

Juice of half a lemon

Salt and pepper, to taste

125 g smoked salmon, cut into 4 strips, each about 12 × 9 cm

Lemon wedges, to garnish

Serves 2

Roasted Red Pepper Dip

2 large red peppers, halved

125 g quark or reduced-fat soft cheese

2 teaspoons sweet chilli sauce

Salt and pepper, to taste

Serves 2–3

This delicious red pepper dip is ideal for serving with crudités, but for a tasty, nutritious lunchtime snack, it can be spread on wholemeal bread and topped with a few salad leaves or alfalfa sprouts.

1 Preheat the oven to 200°C, gas mark 6. Put the pepper halves cut-side down on a large baking sheet and roast for 25–30 minutes, or until the skins are blackened. Leave to cool slightly then put into a polythene bag for 10 minutes, until the skins loosen. Peel away the skin, chop the flesh roughly and set aside.

2 Place the peppers, quark or soft cheese, chilli sauce and seasoning into a food processor or blender and process for 1–2 minutes, until smooth.

3 Cover and place in the fridge for at least 2 hours before serving to allow the flavours to develop.

Tzatziki

½ large cucumber

200 ml Greek yogurt

1 clove garlic, peeled and finely chopped

Salt and pepper, to taste

Serves 2–3

Tzatziki makes a delicious lower-fat alternative to creamy dips and sauces. Serve with vegetable crudités and strips of warm pitta bread.

1 Slice the cucumber in half lengthways. Deseed and dice the flesh.

2 Mix the yogurt, cucumber, garlic and seasoning together. Cover and set aside until needed.

Creamy Guacamole

4 ripe avocados

3 plum tomatoes, skinned, deseeded and diced

Juice of 1 lime

1 clove garlic, peeled and finely chopped

6 tablespoons Greek yogurt

1 large red chilli, deseeded and chopped (optional)

2 tablespoons fresh coriander, chopped

Salt and pepper, to taste

Serves 6

It is essential to use ripe avocados when making guacamole – they should 'give' slightly when pressed at the pointed end. A hard, under-ripe fruit will ripen in 1–2 days at room temperature, if stored in a bowl with ripe fruit. Serve with ready-made tortilla chips and crisp vegetable sticks.

1 Cut the avocados in half and remove the stones. Using a spoon, scoop the flesh into a bowl and mash thoroughly.

2 Add the tomatoes, lime juice, garlic, yogurt, red chilli (if using), coriander and seasoning. Cover the bowl with clingfilm to prevent discolouring, making sure there are no gaps. Chill for 1–2 hours.

3 Uncover and mix lightly once more before serving.

3

Light
Snacks &
Lunches

It's easy to resort to ready-made, processed foods when we want a snack, but these often contain many unwanted additives and very few vitamins and minerals. This chapter offers quick and easy-to-prepare snacks and lunches that are both appealing and healthy.

HUMOUS

400 g can chickpeas, drained and rinsed

2 tablespoons lemon juice

I teaspoon ground cumin

50 ml extra virgin olive oil, plus extra for drizzling

2 cloves garlic, peeled

4 tablespoons tahini

Cayenne pepper, for dusting

Vegetable crudités or toasted pitta bread, to serve

Serves 4

Home-made humous is quick and easy to prepare and knocks spots off the shop-bought variety. Cans of chickpeas are a nutritious and versatile store cupboard ingredient – apart from using them to make humous, you can add them to salads, soups, stews and casseroles.

1 Put the chickpeas in a food processor or blender and process until semi-smooth. Add the lemon juice, cumin, oil, garlic and tahini and continue to blend until smooth. If the mixture is too thick, add a little more oil.

2 Place the mixture in a bowl, spoon over a little extra virgin oil and dust with cayenne or paprika. Serve immediately with vegetable crudités or toasted pitta, or cover and chill until needed.

RED PEPPER HUMOUS

2 large red peppers

400 g can chickpeas, drained and rinsed

2 tablespoons lemon juice

I teaspoon sweet chilli sauce

50 ml extra virgin olive oil

2 cloves garlic, peeled

3 tablespoons tahini

3 tablespoons hot water

Serves 4

The roasted red peppers give this humous a tangy sweet taste, which is enhanced by the chilli sauce. This is delicious served with vegetable crudités or spread on wholemeal bread.

1 Halve the peppers and place under a hot grill for about 20 minutes or until the skins are black. Cover with a clean wet cloth, or place in a plastic bag, and allow to cool for about 10 minutes. Remove the skin from the peppers and blot dry with absorbent kitchen paper.

2 Place the peppers, chickpeas, lemon juice, sweet chilli sauce, olive oil, garlic, tahini and hot water in a food processor or blender and process until smooth. Serve immediately, or cover and chill until needed.

FALAFEL WITH SALAD IN PITTA

Chickpeas are a useful source of fibre, B vitamins and minerals. This recipe makes a hearty and nutritious lunch time snack.

1 Preheat the oven to 180°C, gas mark 4. To make the falafel, mash the chickpeas with the onion and garlic to form a thick pulp. Add the tahini, egg, breadcrumbs, coriander, cumin and salt and mix together well.

2 Divide the falafel mixture into 18 small balls and bake on a baking sheet for 15–20 minutes, or until lightly golden and firm to the touch.

3 To serve, toast the pitta breads, leave to cool slightly and split open. Fill with the shredded lettuce, cherry tomatoes and cucumber. Top the salad with 3 falafel per pitta and drizzle over a little humous, if you like. Sprinkle with a little cayenne pepper or paprika.

FOR THE FALAFEL

400 g can chickpeas, drained and rinsed

1 red onion, roughly chopped

1 clove garlic, peeled and crushed

3 tablespoons tahini

1 egg, beaten

100 g fresh white breadcrumbs

2 tablespoons fresh coriander, chopped

1 teaspoon ground cumin

½ teaspoon salt

TO SERVE

6 large pitta breads

Shredded cos lettuce leaves

Cherry tomatoes, halved

½ cucumber, sliced

Humous (see recipe page 34)

Cayenne pepper or paprika, for sprinkling

Serves 6

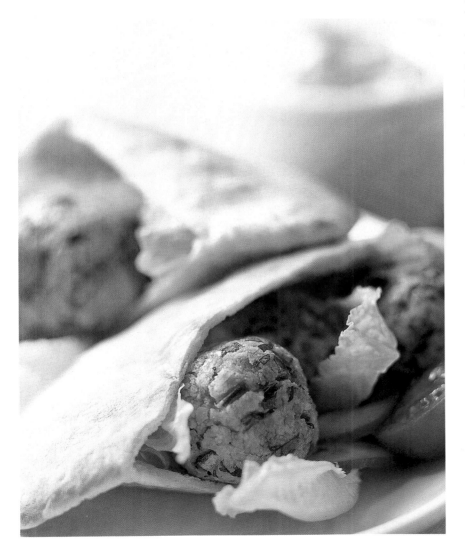

QUICK CIABATTA PIZZA

4 ciabatta rolls

3 tablespoons sun-dried tomato paste
or red pesto

1 tablespoon fresh basil leaves, chopped

3 plum tomatoes, thinly sliced

285 g jar artichoke hearts in oil, drained
and roughly chopped

125 g soft rindless goat's cheese,
crumbled

1 tablespoon hazelnuts, chopped

Black pepper, to taste

Olive oil, for drizzling

Fresh basil leaves, to garnish

Serves 4

*A quick and healthy lunch time snack or light supper dish, this can be
served on its own or accompanied by a fresh green salad.*

1 Preheat the oven to 200°C, gas mark 6. Cut the ciabatta rolls in half and
   arrange cut-side up on a baking sheet.

2 Spread the sun-dried tomato paste or red pesto over the cut surface of each
   toasted roll. Sprinkle over the chopped basil. Place a layer of tomato slices
   over the pesto and basil, then top with artichoke hearts and goat's cheese.
   Sprinkle over the hazelnuts. Season well with black pepper and drizzle
   with a little olive oil.

3 Bake in the oven for about 10 minutes, or until heated through. Garnish
   with basil leaves.

CROQUE MONSIEUR

2 slices white or wholemeal bread

15 g butter

1 slice good quality ham

50 g slice Gruyère cheese

Salt and pepper, to taste

2 teaspoons vegetable oil

Serves 1

*This quick snack is great served with a simple mixed salad. If cooking
for two people, double all the ingredients except the oil – if necessary,
use two pans or cook in batches.*

1 Cut the crusts off the bread, then spread one side of each with some of the
   butter. Place the ham on the buttered side of one slice of bread, cutting to
   fit if necessary, and cover with the Gruyère cheese. Season and top with the
   remaining slice of bread, buttered side down.

2 Press the sandwich together firmly, then cut into 4 triangles.

3 Melt the remaining butter with the oil in a non-stick frying pan. Fry the
   triangles over a moderate heat, turning once, until golden on both sides.
   Press with a fish slice to keep the sandwiches together. Serve hot.

WELSH RAREBIT

Place 50 g grated Cheddar cheese, 15 g butter, 1 tablespoon brown ale,
½ teaspoon mustard and seasoning in a saucepan. Heat very gently, stirring
continuously, until the mixture becomes thick and creamy. Lightly toast one
side of a slice of bread. Pour the sauce over the uncooked side and cook under
a preheated hot grill until it is golden and bubbling. Serve with a crisp green
salad. For buck rarebit, top with a poached egg.

PEPPERED SMOKED MACKEREL SPREAD

275 g peppered smoked mackerel fillets

200 g soft cheese with herbs and garlic

2 tablespoons fresh flat-leaf parsley, chopped

Zest and juice of 1 lemon

Serves 4

A quick and easy fish spread made with soft cheese and a hint of lemon. It can be made in advance and frozen, but remember to defrost it thoroughly before serving. Serve with a green salad and toasted Granary bread.

1 Remove the skin from the smoked mackerel along with any small bones. Flake the fish into a bowl.

2 Add the soft cheese, flat-leaf parsley, lemon zest and juice to the fish and mash together with a fork. Spoon the mixture into a serving bowl. Cover and chill until required.

CHICKEN TIKKA SALAD

4 tablespoons natural yogurt

4 tablespoons mayonnaise

4 tablespoons grated cucumber

3 spring onions, finely chopped

2 teaspoons fresh mint, chopped

Salt and pepper, to taste

Mixed green salad leaves

450 g ready-made chicken tikka

Sprigs of fresh mint, to garnish

Serves 4

Mixing the mayonnaise with natural yogurt reduces the fat and boosts the calcium content of this dish. Serve with toasted pitta bread.

1 Mix the yogurt with the mayonnaise, cucumber, spring onions and mint, blending well to make a dressing. Season to taste. Cover and chill until ready to use.

2 Just before serving, arrange the salad leaves on a large serving plate and top with the chicken tikka. Spoon over the cucumber, mint and yogurt dressing and garnish with sprigs of fresh mint.

CHICKEN CAESAR SALAD WITH PARMESAN CRISPS

The Parmesan crisps in this salad provide plenty of calcium. When serving salads, it is best to put the dressing on at the last moment, as this stops the leaves going soggy.

1　To make the croutons, cut the bread roughly into small pieces. Heat the olive oil in a large frying pan. Add the bread pieces and cook over a high heat for 3 minutes, stirring occasionally, until crisp and golden. Set aside to cool.

2　Preheat the oven to 200°C, gas mark 6. On a large baking sheet, make 8 heaped piles of grated Parmesan cheese, spacing them well apart. Bake for about 5 minutes until the cheese melts, then remove from the oven and leave to cool.

3　On a chopping board, shred the chicken into bite-sized pieces. Tear the lettuce into pieces and put into a large bowl, then toss in a little of the Caesar salad dressing.

4　Pile the lettuce onto 4 large plates, and top with the chicken. Scatter with the croutons, then drizzle with the remaining Caesar dressing. Break the Parmesan crisps into pieces and sprinkle over the salad. Season with black pepper.

4 slices black olive ciabatta or French bread

2 tablespoons olive oil

8 tablespoons Parmesan cheese, freshly grated

3 cooked chicken breast fillets

Inside leaves of 1 cos lettuce

4–5 tablespoons ready-made Caesar salad dressing

Black pepper, to taste

Serves 4

CAESAR SALAD ON TOASTED CIABATTA

Mix together 1 thinly sliced red onion, 2 shredded spring onions, 4 halved cherry tomatoes, ¼ sliced cucumber and 1 tablespoon extra virgin olive oil. Season well. Preheat the grill to high. Slice a ciabatta lengthways, then cut the 2 pieces in half and toast for 1–2 minutes. Drizzle a little olive oil onto the toasted ciabatta then place 1 cos lettuce leaf on each piece. Fill each leaf with shredded cooked chicken and the salad mixture. Spoon over the Caesar dressing, top with Parmesan shavings and season with black pepper.

HOME-MADE CAESAR SALAD DRESSING

Put 3 chopped cloves of garlic in a saucepan with 150 ml white wine. Bring to the boil and simmer for 5 minutes. Leave to cool, then put in a food processor or blender with 50 g grated Parmesan cheese, 4 egg yolks, 1 tablespoon Dijon mustard, 2 anchovy fillets and 1 teaspoon white wine vinegar. Blend until well emulsified, then add 300 ml olive oil in a steady stream, until the dressing is smooth. Season well. Store in a jar and keep in the fridge for up to 1 week.

FETA OMELETTE WITH ROCKET & RED PEPPER

4 large eggs, separated

2 tablespoons fresh mixed herbs, chopped

150 g feta cheese, roughly crumbled

Black pepper, to taste

15 g butter

½ 285 g jar red or mixed peppers in oil, drained and sliced

50 g rocket

Serves 2

This light and fluffy cheese omelette makes a quick and tasty dish. Serve with a simple plum tomato salad.

1 Preheat the grill to high. Beat the egg yolks with 3 tablespoons of water, then stir in the herbs, half the feta and plenty of black pepper. In a clean bowl, whisk the egg whites until stiff, then fold into the egg yolk mixture.

2 Over a medium heat, melt the butter in a large non-stick frying pan until foamy, then spoon in the egg mixture. Cook for 3–4 minutes until the underside of the omelette is golden. Remove from the heat and place under the grill for 2–3 minutes, until the top of the omelette is lightly brown.

3 Scatter the pepper slices and the remaining feta evenly over the top of the omelette. Return to the grill and cook for a further 2–3 minutes until the feta begins to melt slightly. Place the rocket evenly over the top of the red pepper and feta and season with black pepper.

4 Fold the omelette in half, then cut in half and serve.

TWICE-BAKED GOAT'S CHEESE SOUFFLES

40 g butter, plus extra for greasing

25 g Parmesan cheese, freshly grated, plus extra for sprinkling

25 g self-raising flour

225 ml semi-skimmed milk

2 medium eggs, separated

125 g soft rindless goat's cheese, crumbled

Salt and pepper, to taste

Serves 4

These light and tasty soufflés can be served with a crisp green salad and some wholemeal bread for a healthy lunch time snack. They also make a good first course at a dinner party.

1 Lightly grease four 150 ml ramekins and sprinkle Parmesan cheese over the base and the sides of the ramekins until evenly coated.

2 Preheat the oven to 180°C, gas mark 4. Melt the butter in a saucepan, then stir in the flour and cook for 1 minute, stirring constantly. Gradually stir in the milk. Bring to the boil and cook for 2–3 minutes, or until the sauce becomes thick and smooth.

3 Allow the sauce to cool slightly then beat in the egg yolks, goat's cheese and seasoning. Whisk the egg whites until they form soft peaks, then, using a metal spoon, carefully fold into the cheese sauce.

4 Divide the mixture between the ramekins and place in a roasting tin. Pour in enough boiling water to reach halfway up the sides of the ramekins and place in the oven for 20–25 minutes, or until the soufflés are firm to the touch and lightly browned. Remove from the roasting tin and allow to cool. Run a knife around the edge of each soufflé and carefully turn out. Chill until ready to serve.

5 About 30 minutes before serving, heat the oven to 200°C, gas mark 6. Carefully transfer the soufflés to a lightly greased baking sheet, sprinkle with Parmesan cheese and bake for 15–20 minutes or until golden brown.

BLUE CHEESE SOUFFLES
Replace the goat's cheese with Stilton or another blue cheese.

SPINACH & ROQUEFORT PANCAKES

125 g plain flour, sieved

1 egg, beaten

Pinch of salt

300 ml semi–skimmed milk

Vegetable oil, for frying

500 g fresh spinach, washed

225 g Roquefort or other blue cheese, chopped into small pieces

Serves 4 (makes 8 small pancakes)

You can use any strong-tasting cheese to make these pancakes, but the combination of salty Roquefort and spinach works particularly well.

1   Mix the flour, egg and salt together in a large bowl. Gradually beat in enough milk to make a smooth batter with the consistency of single cream.

2   Heat a small pancake pan. When the pan is hot, brush with a little oil and pour in enough batter to thinly coat the base of the pan. Cook over a medium heat for about 1 minute, or until the edges are curling away from the pan and the underside is golden. Using a palette knife, flip the pancake and cook for a further 30 seconds, then turn out onto a sheet of greaseproof paper. Add a little more oil to the pan and repeat the process until all the batter has been used. Cover the pancakes to keep them warm.

3   Place the spinach in a large saucepan with 1 tablespoon of water. Cover and cook until the leaves are just wilted. Transfer to a colander and squeeze out any excess liquid, then chop roughly. Return to the pan and gently reheat.

4   Spoon a little of the spinach into the middle of each of the pancakes and sprinkle over a little of the cheese. Fold the pancakes in half to serve.

CAJUN CHEESE POTATO SKINS WITH TOMATO & RED ONION SALAD

FOR THE POTATO SKINS

4 baking potatoes

Oil, for brushing

2 tablespoons Cajun seasoning mix

8 thin slices of Cheddar cheese, cut in half

These are guaranteed to be a big hit with the whole family. Served with a salad, they are ideal for a light lunch, or with grilled chicken or fish for a more substantial meal.

1   Preheat the oven to 200°C, gas mark 6. Push a metal skewer through each potato (this speeds up the cooking process by about 20 minutes) and bake for 1 hour or until tender.

2   Remove the potatoes from the oven and set aside to cool slightly. Turn the oven up to 225°C, gas mark 7. Remove the skewers and carefully cut each potato into 6 wedges.

3   Brush each potato wedge with a little oil, then dust on both sides with the Cajun seasoning. Put the wedges on a baking sheet and return to the oven for a further 15–20 minutes, until crispy and golden.

4   Meanwhile, make the salad. Slice the tomatoes thinly and place in a shallow dish with the garlic and onion. Whisk the red wine vinegar and

olive oil together, season to taste, then drizzle over the tomato salad. Set aside. Break the radicchio into small pieces, cover and set aside.

5   Remove the potato wedges from the oven and turn the oven off. Arrange the slices of cheese over the wedges and return to the warm oven for 3–4 minutes, or until the cheese has melted.

6   Divide the potato wedges between 4 serving plates with a large spoonful of the tomato and red onion salad and a large handful of the radicchio. Season with a grinding of pepper before serving.

HOME-MADE CAJUN SEASONING

If preferred, you can make your own Cajun seasoning. In a pestle and mortar, pound together 2 tablespoons ground paprika, 2 tablespoons cayenne pepper, 1 tablespoon black pepper, 2 tablespoons garlic granules, 2 tablespoons onion flakes, 1 tablespoon dried oregano, 1 tablespoon dried thyme and 1 tablespoon salt, until you have a powdery consistency. This seasoning can be stored in an airtight jar for up to 3 months.

FOR THE SALAD

4 plum tomatoes

2 cloves garlic, peeled and finely chopped

1 red onion, finely chopped

1 tablespoon red wine vinegar

4 tablespoons extra virgin olive oil

Salt and pepper, to taste

1 head radicchio

Serves 4

BACON & RICOTTA TART

175 g strong plain four, sieved, plus extra for dusting

1 level teaspoon easy-blend dried yeast

1 level teaspoon salt

½ teaspoon sugar

1 tablespoon olive oil

200 g ricotta cheese

150 ml soured cream

1 medium white onion, thinly sliced

Salt and pepper, to taste

8 rashers lean smoked bacon, roughly chopped

Olive oil, for drizzling

Serves 2–4

This makes a tasty meal when served with a rocket salad. It is also perfect for a packed lunch or picnic. If time is short, you could use a ready-made pizza base.

1 To make the dough, place the flour, yeast, salt and sugar in a warm bowl. Mix in the olive oil with 125 ml hand-hot water to make a soft dough. Knead the dough on a floured work surface for 3–4 minutes. Return the dough to the bowl, cover with clingfilm and leave in a warm place to rise for about 1 hour.

2 Meanwhile, to make the topping, mix the ricotta cheese, soured cream and onion together. Add a little salt and plenty of pepper. Preheat the oven to 230°C, gas mark 8 and preheat a baking tray.

3 Once the dough has doubled in size, turn out on to a floured surface. Knead the dough for a couple of minutes to "knock out" the air. Shape the dough into a circle about 25 cm in diameter.

4 Place the dough on the baking tray, spoon over the ricotta mixture, scatter over the bacon and drizzle with olive oil. Cook for 20 minutes or until the bacon is crisp.

SWEET POTATO WITH COTTAGE CHEESE & CRISPY BACON

Although it's low in fat, cottage cheese still provides useful amounts of calcium. Adding a little crispy bacon helps to perk up its flavour.

1　Preheat the oven to 200°C, gas mark 6. Pierce the potato in several places and wrap in foil. Bake in the oven for 45–60 minutes, or until soft.

2　Cook the bacon under a hot grill until crispy. Chop into small pieces and mix into the cottage cheese.

3　Remove the potato from the foil and slice in half. Spoon over the cottage cheese and bacon mixture and serve.

1 medium sweet potato, about 250 g

2 rashers lean smoked bacon

100 g cottage cheese

Serves 1

SPINACH & POTATO CAKE

Served with a simple tomato salad, this dish makes a healthy and satisfying lunch on a cold day.

1　Preheat the oven to 180°C, gas mark 4. Melt the butter in a large saucepan, add the garlic and spinach and cook until the spinach is just wilted. Drain well and chop roughly.

2　Mix together the spinach, eggs, crème fraîche, milk, 75 g of the Gruyère cheese and the herbs. Season with salt, pepper and nutmeg.

3　Lightly grease a 23 cm springform cake tin. Cover the base with a layer of sliced potatoes, then a layer of the spinach mixture. Continue layering, finishing with layer of potatoes. Sprinkle with the remaining Gruyère cheese and cover the tin with lightly greased foil. Place in a roasting tin and pour in enough boiling water to reach halfway up the sides of the cake tin.

4　Bake for 1½ hours until the potatoes are tender – remove the foil for the last 15 minutes to allow the top to brown. Allow to cool in the tin for 5–10 minutes before serving.

15 g butter, plus extra for greasing

1 clove garlic, peeled and finely chopped

500 g fresh spinach, washed

3 eggs, beaten

2 x 200 ml cartons reduced-fat crème fraîche

2 tablespoons semi-skimmed milk

125 g Gruyère cheese, grated

3 tablespoons fresh mixed herbs, chopped

Salt and pepper, to taste

Pinch freshly grated nutmeg

4 large potatoes, peeled and thinly sliced

Serves 6

4 Main Courses

This chapter features meat, fish and vegetarian main courses, ranging from those suitable for a quick family meal to ideas for a more elaborate dinner party. Most importantly, all the dishes provide essential vitamins and minerals for strong, healthy bones.

BRIE-STUFFED CHICKEN WITH CREAMY PESTO

4 boneless, skinless chicken breasts

200 g Brie

8 slices Parma ham

Vegetable oil, for frying

2 tablespoons green pesto

2 tablespoons Greek yogurt

Serves 4

Mixing Greek yogurt into the pesto gives it a wonderfully creamy flavour and helps to boost the calcium content of this dish. Serve with lightly steamed vegetables and new potatoes.

1 Cut sideways into each chicken breast to create a pocket. Cut the Brie into 4 slices and stuff one into each piece of chicken. Wrap 2 slices of Parma ham around each piece and secure with cocktail sticks.

2 Place the chicken on a lightly oiled baking tray and cook in the oven at 190°C, gas mark 5 for 35 minutes, or until the chicken is cooked through.

3 Remove the cocktail sticks and transfer the chicken to a warm plate. Mix the pesto and yogurt together in a small bowl and drizzle the mixture over the cooked chicken.

FRESH PESTO

Place 50 g fresh basil, 2 crushed cloves garlic, 2 tablespoons pine nuts, 125 ml olive oil and 50 g freshly grated Parmesan cheese in a blender or food processor and purée until smooth. The fresh pesto will keep for up to 2 weeks in the fridge.

CHICKEN & WILD MUSHROOM STROGANOFF

Packets of fresh wild mushrooms can be found in supermarkets, but, if not, you can simply double the amount of chestnut mushrooms. Serve with plain boiled rice or boiled new potatoes.

1   Cut the chicken into thin strips. Heat the butter and oil in a large deep non-stick frying pan or casserole dish until it foams. Add half the chicken and stir-fry over a high heat for 4–5 minutes until tender and lightly browned. Remove with a slotted spoon and drain on kitchen paper. Set aside. Repeat with the remaining chicken and set aside.

2   Add the onion, mushrooms and red pepper to the frying pan or casserole dish and season well. Sauté over a medium heat for 5 minutes until the onion is soft. Add the tomato purée and cook for 1 minute. Add the stock and sour cream or crème fraîche and stir well. Simmer for about 5 minutes until the mixture thickens slightly.

3   Return the chicken to the dish and simmer for 2–3 minutes to heat through. To serve, divide between 4 warmed plates and sprinkle with snipped chives.

4 boneless, skinless chicken breasts

25 g butter

1 tablespoon olive oil

2 medium red onions, cut into wedges

125 g mixed wild mushrooms, sliced

125 g chestnut mushrooms, sliced

1 red pepper, deseeded and sliced

Salt and pepper, to taste

2 tablespoons sun-dried tomato purée

240 ml chicken stock

150 ml sour cream or crème fraîche

2 tablespoons fresh chives, snipped

Serves 4

GARLIC CHICKEN IN YOGURT

The yogurt and almonds boost the calcium content of this spiced chicken dish. Serve with plain boiled basmati rice.

1   Mix the chilli flakes, cinnamon, 2 tablespoons olive oil, garlic and curry paste together and season well. In a shallow dish, toss the chicken pieces with the curry paste mixture. Cover and leave for 20 minutes.

2   Heat the remaining oil in a large non-stick frying pan. Stir-fry the chicken for 4–5 minutes until tender and lightly browned.

3   Stir in the ground almonds and yogurt and heat through for 2–3 minutes. Sprinkle over the garam masala and coriander and serve immediately.

1 teaspoon crushed chilli flakes

1 teaspoon ground cinnamon

3 tablespoons olive oil

4 cloves garlic, peeled and finely crushed

2 teaspoons hot curry paste

Salt and pepper, to taste

350 g chicken breast fillets, cut into bite-sized pieces

100 g ground almonds, toasted

340 ml Greek yogurt

1 teaspoon garam masala

2 tablespoons fresh coriander, chopped

Serves 4

CORONATION CHICKEN SALAD

Originally created for the Queen's coronation by the Cordon Bleu Cookery School, this is a more contemporary version. It is ideal for using up left-over cooked chicken, and makes a great sandwich filling.

FOR THE CHICKEN

50 g butter

1 medium onion, finely chopped

8 ready-to-eat dried apricots, finely chopped

Small pinch saffron strands

Zest of 1 lemon

2 tablespoons runny honey

2 tablespoons hot curry paste

200 ml dry white wine

8 tablespoons mayonnaise

8 tablespoons Greek yogurt

450 g skinless, boneless cooked chicken, cut into bite-sized pieces

2 tablespoons fresh coriander, chopped

Salt and pepper, to taste

FOR THE SALAD

1 red pepper, thinly sliced

1 red chilli, deseeded and thinly sliced

4 spring onions, cut into thin strips

50 g unsalted peanuts, chopped

Wild rocket, to garnish

Fresh coriander sprigs, to garnish

Serves 4–6

1 Melt the butter in a saucepan and cook the onion for 5 minutes until soft. Add the apricots, saffron, lemon zest, honey, curry paste and wine. Simmer uncovered for 25 minutes or until the mixture is the consistency of thin chutney. Leave to cool.

2 Mix the mayonnaise with the yogurt, add the chicken and the cooled curry mixture and mix well. Add the coriander and season to taste.

3 To make the salad, mix together the pepper, chilli, spring onions and peanuts. Divide the chicken between 4–6 plates and top with the salad mixture. Serve with rocket leaves and more coriander.

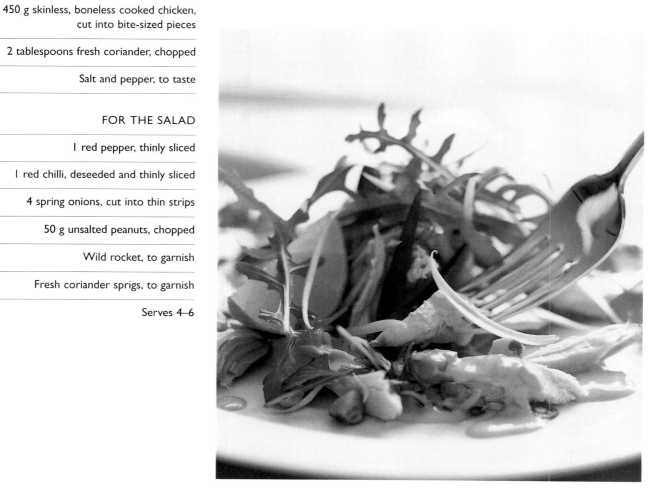

CHICKEN & SESAME BITES

Everyone will love these tasty little chicken bites. Sesame seeds have a deliciously nutty flavour and are a useful source of calcium, particularly for people who don't eat dairy products. Serve with a spicy tomato salsa.

1　Mix together the breadcrumbs, sesame seeds and seasoning, then spread over a large plate or baking tray.

2　Dip the chicken pieces into the beaten egg then roll in the breadcrumb and sesame seed mixture until thoroughly coated. Carefully lay the chicken on a lightly greased baking sheet and place in the fridge for 30 minutes.

3　Meanwhile, preheat the oven to 200°C, gas mark 6. Spray the chicken with olive oil and bake for 10–15 minutes, until the breadcrumbs are golden brown and the chicken cooked through.

75 g fine white breadcrumbs

75 g sesame seeds

Salt and pepper, to taste

2 large skinless chicken breasts, cut into bite-sized pieces

1 egg, beaten

Extra virgin olive oil spray

Serves 4

QUICK TURKEY CASSOULET

This is a hearty and wholesome supper dish guaranteed to warm you up on a cold day. Turkey is a useful source of zinc, which is helpful in building strong bones. Serve with a crisp green salad.

1　Heat 2 tablespoons of the oil in a large non-stick saucepan. Add the onion, garlic, bacon and celery and cook over a low heat for 10 minutes, stirring occasionally.

2　Add the tomatoes, chicken stock and soy sauce. Bring to the boil, then reduce to a fast simmer and cook for about 15 minutes, or until the sauce begins to thicken.

3　Add the mustard, beans and turkey and continue to cook for a further 5 minutes. Transfer the mixture into a shallow ovenproof dish.

4　Mix the breadcrumbs, Parmesan cheese and parsley together and sprinkle over the turkey mixture. Drizzle with the remaining tablespoon of olive oil and place under a medium–hot grill for 5 minutes, or until the breadcrumbs are golden brown.

3 tablespoons olive oil

1 medium red onion, finely chopped

2 cloves garlic, crushed or finely chopped

125 g smoked back bacon, roughly chopped

2 sticks celery, finely chopped

400 g can chopped tomatoes

250 ml chicken stock

2 tablespoons dark soy sauce

2 teaspoons Dijon mustard

2 x 400 g cans mixed beans, rinsed and drained

400 g cooked turkey, roughly chopped

75 g fresh white breadcrumbs

50 g Parmesan cheese, freshly grated

3 tablespoons parsley, chopped

Serves 4

PORK STUFFED WITH APRICOTS & PINE NUTS

Apricots are rich in potassium, which is beneficial for strong bones. They also provide useful amounts of calcium. Serve this for Sunday lunch with potatoes and green vegetables.

FOR THE STUFFING

1 tablespoon olive oil

1 medium onion, peeled and finely chopped

40 g fresh white breadcrumbs

40 g ready-to-eat dried apricots, roughly chopped

25 g pine nuts, lightly toasted

2 tablespoons fresh parsley, chopped

Salt and pepper, to taste

1 small egg, beaten

FOR THE PORK

1 pork loin, about 900 g, trimmed

1 tablespoon olive oil

100 ml white wine

FOR THE GRAVY

2 teaspoons plain flour

400 ml chicken stock

3 tablespoons Greek yogurt

1 tablespoon wholegrain mustard

Salt and pepper, to taste

Serves 4–6

1 Preheat the oven to 180°C, gas mark 4. To make the stuffing, heat the olive oil in a non-stick pan and fry the onion for 4–5 minutes until soft. In a large bowl, mix together the breadcrumbs, apricots, pine nuts, parsley and seasoning. Add the cooked onion and the egg and mix well.

2 Split the pork almost in half, down the length of the loin, and spread the stuffing in the middle. Bring the two cut edges of pork together to enclose the stuffing and tie at intervals with string. Heat the oil in a pan, wait until it is hot, then add the pork and brown on all sides. Transfer the pork to a roasting tin, cut side down. Pour over the wine and cook in the oven for 1 hour. Test that the pork is cooked by piercing the thickest part with a fine skewer – the juices should run clear. Transfer to a warm plate, cover with foil and keep warm while you make the gravy.

3 Put the roasting tin on the hob and stir the flour into the juices from the meat. Gradually stir in the stock and simmer for 5 minutes, until the gravy begins to thicken. Stir in the yogurt and mustard and season to taste. Slice the pork and serve with the gravy.

PORK STUFFED WITH APPLE & WALNUTS

For an alternative stuffing, you can replace the apricots with 40 g dried apple and the pine nuts with 25 g roughly chopped walnuts. To make the gravy use 200 ml chicken stock and 200 ml dry cider.

PORK WITH PAK CHOI & BLACK BEAN SAUCE

2 tablespoons vegetable oil

450 g pork tenderloin, thinly sliced

2 cloves garlic, crushed or finely chopped

2.5 cm fresh ginger, finely chopped

8 spring onions, cut into 0.5 cm slices

125 g shiitake mushrooms

200 g broccoli florets

125 g baby sweetcorn, sliced lengthways

190 g black bean sauce

1 tablespoon runny honey

150 g pak choi, trimmed and sliced

200 g egg noodles

1 tablespoon sesame oil

Spring onions, thinly sliced, to garnish

Serves 4

Pak choi has a mild and pleasant flavour and a crisp texture. If you can't find pak choi, you can use Chinese cabbage instead.

1   Heat 1 tablespoon of the vegetable oil in a wok or large frying pan. Add the pork and stir-fry over a high heat for 5 minutes, or until browned. Remove from the pan and set aside.

2   Wipe the wok clean with kitchen paper and heat the remaining vegetable oil. Once the oil is hot, add the garlic, ginger and spring onions and stir-fry for 1 minute. Add the mushrooms, broccoli and sweetcorn and continue cooking for 2–3 minutes.

3   Return the pork to the wok, stir in the black bean sauce, honey, pak choi and 150 ml water. Cook for a further 5 minutes or until the sauce is hot.

4   Meanwhile, cook the noodles according to the manufacturer's instructions. Drain well, then stir through the sesame oil. To serve, place the noodles and pork stir-fry in a bowl and garnish with spring onions.

PORK ESCALOPES WITH CELERIAC CREAM MASH

FOR THE MASH

450 g celeriac, peeled and cut into even-sized pieces

450 g potatoes, peeled and cut into even-sized pieces

Small knob butter

3 spring onions, finely chopped

150 ml crème fraîche

Salt and pepper, to taste

The dense texture of celeriac makes a delicious creamy mash, which provides an excellent accompaniment to plain meats, such as pork.

1   Bring a large pan of salted water to the boil. Add the celeriac and potato, bring back to the boil and cook for 20–30 minutes, or until both are tender. Drain well, return to the pan and mash.

2   In a small pan, heat the butter and cook the spring onions for 2–3 minutes, until soft. Add the crème fraîche and warm through for 1 minute. Add the mixture to the mash, beat well and season. Cover and keep warm until ready to serve.

3 Meanwhile, put the escalopes between two sheets of greaseproof paper and thin by beating with a rolling pin. Brush each escalope with the melted butter and coat both sides with the breadcrumbs.

4 Heat the grill to medium. Arrange the breaded escalopes on a foil-lined grill rack and grill for 3–4 minutes on each side.

5 Serve the escalopes on warm serving plates with a large spoonful of the celeriac mash. Garnish with sage leaves and freshly ground black pepper.

FOR THE ESCALOPES

4 pork escalopes, each about 125 g

25 g butter, melted

50 g fine white breadcrumbs

Fresh sage leaves, to garnish

Freshly ground black pepper

Serves 4

POLENTA WITH BACON & MUSHROOMS

Polenta, which is made from cornmeal, is a speciality of northern Italy. For a change, you could replace the Parmesan with a blue cheese, such as Stilton, or goat's cheese.

175 g quick-cook polenta

125 g Parmesan cheese, freshly grated

3 tablespoons fresh mixed herbs, roughly chopped

15 g butter

Salt, to taste

1 tablespoon olive oil

225 g rindless smoked back bacon, roughly chopped

8 spring onions, chopped

300 g mixed mushrooms, roughly chopped

300 ml chicken stock

Salt and pepper, to taste

6 tablespoons Greek yogurt

Serves 4

1 Place 700 ml of salted water in a large non-stick saucepan and bring to the boil. Pour in the polenta in a slow steady stream, stirring continuously. Reduce the heat and cook for 1 minute, or until the polenta is thick. Remove from the heat, stir in the Parmesan cheese, herbs and butter and more salt, if required.

2 Spread the polenta into a shallow lightly oiled tin, to a thickness of about 1 cm. Allow to cool, then cut into triangles.

3 Heat the oil in a large non-stick frying pan. Add the bacon and cook over a high heat for 5 minutes, until it begins to brown. Add the spring onions and mushrooms and continue to cook for a further 5 minutes. Add the stock, season to taste and reduce the heat slightly. Cook for 20–30 minutes or until the liquid has reduced. Stir in the yogurt.

4 Place the polenta triangles under a preheated grill for 3–4 minutes, turn and continue to cook for a further 3 minutes. Transfer to warm plates, spoon over the bacon and mushroom mixture and serve.

MUSHROOM POLENTA

This recipe can be adapted for vegetarians by simply omitting the bacon and using vegetable stock instead of chicken stock.

BROCCOLI & SMOKED HAM TAGLIATELLE

*If you do not have fresh pasta, dried pasta can also be used in this dish
– pasta shells work particularly well. Serve with a crisp green salad.*

1   Cook the pasta in boiling salted water for 3–4 minutes, according to the packet instructions, until *al dente*.

2   Meanwhile, melt the butter in a large saucepan, add the onion, broccoli and yellow pepper and fry for 5–7 minutes until just softened. Stir in the mascarpone cheese and heat through for 1–2 minutes until soft. Add the smoked ham, grated nutmeg and flat-leaf parsley.

3   Fold the pasta into the sauce, season to taste and heat through for 1–2 minutes. Heat the grill to high. Turn the pasta into a shallow heatproof dish, sprinkle with Cheddar cheese and grill until golden and bubbling.

VEGETABLE TAGLIATELLE
For a delicious vegetarian alternative, omit the ham and replace with 225 g mixture of any vegetables that can be cooked quickly, such as mange tout, mushrooms or leeks.

225 g fresh green or white tagliatelle

25 g butter

1 large onion, halved and sliced

225 g small broccoli florets

1 yellow pepper, deseeded and chopped

250 g mascarpone cheese

225 g smoked ham, shredded

½ teaspoon grated nutmeg

2 tablespoons flat-leaf parsley, chopped

Salt and pepper, to taste

125 g Cheddar cheese, grated

Serves 4

SKEWERED LAMB WITH TOMATO, CHILLI & YOGURT MARINADE

FOR THE LAMB

700 g lamb neck fillet, trimmed and cut into chunks

1 tablespoon olive oil

2 cloves garlic, crushed

3 small red chillies, deseeded and finely chopped

25 g sun-dried tomatoes in oil, drained and finely chopped

2 teaspoons balsamic vinegar

Pinch soft brown sugar

100 ml natural yogurt

Freshly ground black pepper, to taste

These tender marinated chunks of lamb are delicious served with basmati rice. Look out for small jars of chopped chillies in sunflower oil, as this speeds up the preparation and avoids the need to handle fresh chillies, which can be off-putting for some people.

1 Place the lamb, oil, garlic, chillies, sun-dried tomatoes, balsamic vinegar, brown sugar and yogurt together in a shallow bowl and stir well. Season with freshly ground black pepper. Cover, place in the fridge and leave to marinate for at least 3 hours, or preferably overnight. Soak 4 wooden skewers in cold water for 30 minutes before using.

2 To make the rice, bring a large pan of water to the boil, stir in the rice and add a pinch of salt. Return to the boil, cover and simmer for 12–14 minutes, or cook according to the manufacturer's instructions. Drain well. Stir in the chopped coriander and sun-dried tomatoes.

3 Heat the grill to high. Thread the lamb onto the skewers, reserving the marinade. Put the skewered lamb on a grill rack and grill for 3–4 minutes on each side for rare, or 5–6 minutes on each side for well done. Brush with the reserved marinade during grilling.

4 Serve the lamb on the skewers with the rice. Garnish with lime wedges and coriander sprigs.

FOR THE RICE

250 g easy-cook basmati rice

Pinch of salt

2 tablespoons fresh coriander, chopped

1 tablespoon sun-dried tomatoes in oil, drained and finely chopped

Lime wedges, to garnish

Fresh coriander sprigs, to garnish

Serves 4

GARLIC & CUMIN ROASTED LAMB WITH APRICOT & CHICKPEA SALSA

Here, roast lamb is given an unusual twist when served with a tangy salsa. The salsa can be made in advance and stored, covered, in the fridge until ready to serve – remove from the fridge while cooking the lamb to allow the flavours to develop.

1 Preheat the oven to 200°C, gas mark 6. Rub the cumin seeds over the lamb fillets. Using a small sharp knife, make small cuts all over the fillets and insert the garlic slivers.

2 Put the lamb fillets into a roasting tin and roast in the oven for 30 minutes, until tender.

3 Meanwhile, make the salsa. Combine the red onion, chilli, sun-dried tomatoes, apricots, chickpeas, oil, lime zest and juice and coriander together in a bowl. Cover and set aside.

4 When the lamb is cooked, remove from the oven and leave to stand for 5 minutes. To serve, slice the lamb and top with the salsa. Garnish with mint leaves.

1 teaspoon cumin seeds

6 lamb neck fillets

2 garlic cloves, cut into slivers

FOR THE SALSA

1 small red onion, finely chopped

1 red chilli, deseeded and finely chopped

2 sun-dried tomatoes, finely chopped

125 g ready-to-eat dried apricots, finely chopped

300 g canned chickpeas, drained and rinsed

1 tablespoon olive oil

Zest and juice of 1 lime

1 tablespoon fresh coriander, chopped

Mint leaves, to garnish

Serves 4

MOROCCAN LAMB WITH CHICKPEAS & APRICOTS

2 teaspoons ground ginger

2 teaspoons ground cumin

2 teaspoons paprika

1 cinnamon stick

100 ml orange juice

450 g lamb fillet, cut into bite-sized pieces

1 tablespoon vegetable oil

8 shallots or baby onions, peeled

2 cloves garlic, peeled and crushed

1 tablespoon plain flour

1 tablespoon tomato purée

200 ml chicken stock

150 ml sherry

Salt and pepper, to taste

125 g ready-to-eat dried apricots

400 g can chickpeas, drained and rinsed

Fresh coriander, chopped, to garnish

Serves 4

Here, the lamb is marinated in a tangy, spicy marinade, which gives it a delicious flavour. Both chickpeas and apricots are good sources of calcium, so this dish is great for people on dairy-free diets. Serve with couscous or plain rice.

1 Put the ginger, cumin, paprika and the cinnamon stick in a large bowl and pour over the orange juice. Add the lamb and mix well. Cover and leave in a cool place for at least 1 hour, or preferably overnight.

2 Preheat the oven to 180°C, gas mark 4. Heat the oil in a large flameproof casserole dish. Remove the lamb from the marinade and cook it in the dish over a high heat for 5 minutes until lightly browned. Remove with a slotted spoon and set aside.

3 Lower the heat and add a little more oil if necessary. Cook the onions and garlic for 3 minutes, or until they are just beginning to brown. Return the lamb to the dish, stir in the flour and tomato purée and continue cooking for 1 minute, stirring frequently.

4 Add the remaining marinade, stock, sherry and season to taste. Bring to the boil then reduce the heat, cover and bake in the oven for 1 hour.

5 Add the apricots and chickpeas and return to the oven for a further 15 minutes. Garnish with chopped coriander and serve.

MOROCCAN LAMB WITH BUTTER BEANS & PRUNES
For a change, try replacing the chickpeas with canned butter beans and the apricots with prunes.

MOUSSAKA

The combination of ricotta, Parmesan and Cheddar cheeses makes this warm and comforting dish a real calcium booster. Choose lean minced lamb to help reduce the fat content. Serve with a mixed green salad.

1 Preheat the oven to 180°C, gas mark 4. Heat 1 tablespoon of the oil in a non-stick saucepan, add the onion and garlic and fry for 5 minutes, or until soft.

2 Add the lamb and cook until tender and browned. Add the tomatoes, tomato purée, cinnamon, oregano and seasoning. Bring to the boil and cook over a low heat for about 20 minutes.

3 Place the potato in a large pan of boiling salted water and cook for 5 minutes. Drain well. Brush the aubergine with the remaining oil and place under a hot grill for 4 minutes on each side, until nicely browned.

4 Mix together the ricotta and Parmesan cheeses. Stir in the beaten egg and milk and season to taste.

5 Arrange half of the grilled aubergine over the base of a shallow ovenproof dish. Spoon over the meat sauce, cover with the remaining aubergine and top with the sliced potatoes.

6 Pour over the cheese sauce, sprinkle with the Cheddar cheese and bake in the oven for 30–40 minutes.

2 tablespoons olive oil

1 large red onion, peeled and finely chopped

2 cloves garlic, crushed or finely chopped

450 g lean minced lamb

2 x 400 g cans chopped tomatoes

1 tablespoon sun-dried tomato purée

¼ teaspoon ground cinnamon

1 teaspoon dried oregano

Salt and pepper, to taste

1 large potato, peeled and thinly sliced

1 large aubergine, cut into slices 0.5 cm thick

250 g ricotta cheese

50 g fresh Parmesan cheese, grated

1 egg, beaten

4 tablespoons full-fat milk

25 g Cheddar cheese, grated

Serves 4

SHEPHERD'S PIE

450 g minced lamb

1 large onion, chopped

1 bay leaf

50 g mushrooms, sliced

2 medium carrots, sliced

25 g plain flour

300 ml passata

1 tablespoon sun-dried tomato purée

Salt and pepper, to taste

700 g potatoes, peeled and cut into
even-sized pieces

25 g butter

4 tablespoons full-fat milk

75 g Lancashire cheese, crumbled

Serves 4

*This version has more flavoursome ingredients than many traditional
shepherd's pie recipes and has a delicious cheese topping. Serve with a
steamed green vegetable, such as broccoli.*

1 Dry fry the minced lamb with the onion, bay leaf, mushrooms and carrots
for 8–10 minutes.

2 Add the flour and cook, stirring, for 1 minute. Gradually blend in the
passata and tomato purée. Cook, stirring, until the mixture thickens and
boils. Cover and simmer gently for 25 minutes.

3 Remove the bay leaf and season to taste. Spoon into an ovenproof dish.

4 Heat the oven to 200°C, gas mark 6. Cook the potatoes in boiling salted
water for 20 minutes, until tender. Drain well and mash with the butter
and milk. Spread the mashed potato over the mince mixture and sprinkle
with the crumbled cheese. Bake for 15–20 minutes until golden brown.

BLUE CHEESE & WALNUT STEAKS

125 g Stilton or other blue cheese,
crumbled

25 g butter, softened

50–75 g shelled walnut pieces,
finely chopped

Freshly ground black pepper, to taste

4 sirloin or fillet steaks, each weighing
about 125–180 g, trimmed

Serves 4

*These steaks have a tasty, and unexpectedly crunchy, topping.
Simple accompaniments, such as boiled potatoes and a mixed salad, are
all that are needed to complete this meal.*

1 Put the cheese in a bowl and mash with a fork. Add butter and walnuts
and mix thoroughly. Season to taste with pepper.

2 Preheat the grill to high. Put the steaks on a grill rack and season with
plenty of pepper. Place under the grill and cook for 1–2 minutes on each
side for rare, 4 minutes on each side for medium and 6–7 minutes on
each side for well done.

3 Remove the steaks from under the grill and sprinkle with the cheese and
nut mixture. Press down the mixture with a palette knife. Grill for 1
minute, or until the topping is melted and bubbling. Serve immediately.

MEATBALLS WITH MOZZARELLA & TOMATO SAUCE

The mozzarella cheese melts while the meatballs are cooking to give a deliciously creamy filling. Combined with a rich tomato sauce, this makes a comforting supper, when served with a large plate of spaghetti.

1 To make the meatballs, heat the olive oil in a large non-stick pan. Add the onion and the garlic and cook over a low heat for 5 minutes, until soft. Place the minced beef, breadcrumbs, egg and Parmesan cheese in a bowl. Add the cooked onions and garlic and mix well.

2 Cut or tear the mozzarella cheese into 20 small pieces. Take a heaped tablespoon of the mince mixture and shape into a ball around a piece of mozzarella cheese. Repeat the process with the remaining meat, until you have 20 meatballs. Place the meatballs on a plate or tray and chill for 30 minutes.

3 To make the sauce, heat the oil in a saucepan, add the onion and cook for 4–5 minutes. Add the garlic, tomatoes, tomato purée, mixed herbs, red wine and seasoning. Bring to the boil, reduce the heat, cover and simmer over a low heat for 15 minutes, stirring occasionally. Remove the lid, add the meatballs and continue to cook for a further 20 minutes. Serve the meatballs with the sauce poured over.

FOR THE MEATBALLS

1 tablespoon olive oil

½ small onion, finely chopped

½ clove garlic, peeled and finely chopped

450 g lean minced beef

50 g fine white breadcrumbs

1 egg, beaten

2 tablespoons Parmesan cheese, freshly grated

75 g mozzarella cheese

FOR THE SAUCE

1 tablespoon olive oil

½ small onion, finely chopped

½ clove garlic, peeled and finely chopped

2 x 400 g cans chopped tomatoes

1 tablespoon tomato purée

1 teaspoon dried mixed herbs

150 ml red wine

Salt and pepper, to taste

Serves 4

MINCED BEEF WITH POLENTA TOPPING

Polenta is gluten-free, so this is a good alternative to a pastry-topped pie for anyone who can't eat wheat or gluten. Mixing Parmesan cheese with the polenta helps boost both the flavour and the calcium content. Serve with a green salad.

1 Heat the oil in large non-stick saucepan. Add the onion and garlic and cook for 5 minutes until soft. Add the beef and cook until browned.

2 Stir in the tomatoes, tomato paste, wine and seasoning and bring to the boil. Reduce the heat and simmer gently for 30 minutes.

3 To make the polenta topping, place 700 ml of salted water in a large saucepan and bring to the boil. Pour in the polenta in a slow steady stream, stirring continuously. Reduce the heat to low and cook for 1 minute or until the polenta is thick. Stir in the Parmesan cheese, the sun-dried tomatoes, rosemary and butter and add more salt, if required. Spread the polenta into a shallow lightly oiled tin, to a thickness of about 1 cm. Allow to cool.

4 Once the polenta is cold, cut it into triangles. Heat the oven to 200°C, gas mark 6. Place the beef mixture in a shallow ovenproof dish and arrange the polenta over the top so that the triangles overlap slightly.

5 Sprinkle with Parmesan cheese and bake for 20–30 minutes, until the topping is golden brown.

OLIVE & STILTON POLENTA TOPPING
Adding different flavours to the polenta topping transforms this recipe. Add 50 g pitted, roughly chopped black olives to the polenta and use 150 g crumbled Stilton or another blue cheese instead of the Parmesan.

1 tablespoon olive oil

1 medium red onion, peeled and finely chopped

1 large clove garlic, finely chopped

450 g lean minced beef

2 x 400 g cans chopped tomatoes

2 tablespoons sun-dried tomato paste

200 ml red wine

Salt and pepper, to taste

FOR THE POLENTA TOPPING

100 g quick-cook polenta

75 g Parmesan cheese, freshly grated, plus extra for sprinkling

75 g sun-dried tomatoes, roughly chopped

½ teaspoon fresh rosemary, chopped

10 g butter

Salt, to taste

Vegetable oil, for greasing

Serves 4

SALMON FISH CAKES

550 g floury potatoes, such as Desirée or King Edwards, peeled and cut into large chunks

2 tablespoons mayonnaise

418 g can red salmon, drained

Salt and pepper, to taste

Plain flour, for dusting

1 large egg, beaten

100 g fine white breadcrumbs

4 tablespoons sunflower oil

Lemon wedges, to garnish

Serves 4

Nutritionists recommend that we eat at least two servings of oil-rich fish, such as salmon, a week. As well as providing healthy omega-3 fatty acids, canned salmon, when eaten with the bones, is an excellent source of calcium. Serve the fish cakes with tzatziki and new potatoes.

1   Place the potatoes in a large pan of salted water, bring to the boil and cook for about 20 minutes, until tender. Drain well and mash with the mayonnaise.

2   Place the salmon, including the bones, in a large bowl and mash with a fork. Add the mashed potato and season to taste. Mix well, then cover and place in the fridge for 1 hour.

3   Remove the mixture from the fridge. Shape into 8 fish cakes and dust with flour. Carefully dip each fish cake into the beaten egg, then into the breadcrumbs, making sure it is evenly coated.

4   Heat half the oil in a large non-stick frying pan and cook half the fish cakes over a high heat for 4 minutes each side, until the breadcrumbs are golden brown. Drain on absorbent kitchen paper, then transfer to a warm oven while you cook the remaining fish cakes. Garnish with lemon wedges.

SALMON & LEEK LASAGNE

25 g butter

2 large leeks, washed and thinly sliced

40 g plain flour

600 ml semi-skimmed milk

225 g Cheddar cheese, grated

Salt and pepper, to taste

213 g can pink salmon, drained and flaked

8 sheets fresh lasagne

2 tablespoons sunflower seeds, toasted

Serves 4

Canned salmon provides a useful source of calcium, vitamin D and phosphorus, all of which are essential for strong bones. Serve this lasagne with a large green salad and crusty bread.

1   Preheat the oven to 190°C, gas mark 5. Grease a shallow ovenproof dish.

2   Heat the butter in a large non-stick frying pan, add the leeks and cook for 4–5 minutes until soft.

3   Place the flour and milk in a small saucepan, whisk together, then slowly bring to the boil, stirring continuously. Reduce the heat and simmer for 1 minute. Remove from the heat, stir in half of the cheese and season to taste.

4   Mix the leeks, half of the cheese sauce and the salmon together. Spoon half the salmon and leek mixture into the bottom of the prepared dish and top with a layer of fresh lasagne. Spoon over the remaining salmon mixture, top with a final layer of lasagne and pour over the remaining cheese sauce. Sprinkle with the remaining cheese and the sunflower seeds. Bake in the oven for 20 minutes, until the top is bubbling.

SMOKED SALMON & DILL QUICHE

The sweet aniseed flavour of the dill complements the smoked salmon perfectly in this nourishing, creamy dish.

1 Roll out the pastry on a lightly floured surface and use to line a 23 × 4 cm deep, loose-bottomed flan tin. Place on a baking sheet, cover and chill in the fridge for 30 minutes. Preheat the oven to 200°C, gas mark 6.

2 Prick the base of the flan, line with a large sheet of greaseproof paper and fill with baking beans. Bake for 10–15 minutes, then carefully remove the paper and the beans. Return to the oven for a further 5 minutes until the base is firm to the touch and lightly golden. Remove from the oven and set aside while making the filling.

3 Heat the oil and cook the onion for 5 minutes until soft. Turn down the oven to 170°C, gas mark 3. Whisk the eggs and cheeses together until smooth, then whisk in the cream, dill and pepper. Scatter the onion and salmon over the base of the flan case and pour over the egg mixture.

4 Bake the quiche for 45–55 minutes, until lightly set. Garnish with smoked salmon trimmings and dill sprigs.

225 g ready-made shortcrust pastry

Plain flour, for dusting

1 tablespoon oil

1 large onion, finely chopped

2 eggs

200 g full-fat soft cream cheese

25 g rindless soft goat's cheese

300 ml single cream

1 tablespoon fresh dill, chopped, plus extra to garnish

Pepper, to taste

125 g smoked salmon trimmings, roughly chopped, plus extra to garnish

Serves 6

QUICK SALMON KEDGEREE

225 g basmati rice

2 teaspoons olive oil

4 spring onions, roughly chopped

213 g can salmon, drained, bones and skin removed, then roughly flaked

½ teaspoon coriander seeds, finely crushed

3 tablespoons double cream

3 hard-boiled eggs, quartered

3 tablespoons fresh flat-leaf parsley, chopped, plus extra to garnish

Salt and pepper, to taste

2 lemons, cut into wedges, to garnish

Serves 4

Oil-rich fish, such as salmon, are one of the few dietary sources of vitamin D, which is essential for the absorption of calcium. This delicious rice dish is ideal for brunch.

1   Bring a large pan of salted water to the boil. Stir in the rice and return to the boil, then cover and simmer for 12–14 minutes until just tender. Drain the rice well, rinse with boiling water and drain again.

2   Meanwhile, heat the oil in a large non-stick frying pan and cook the spring onions for 1–2 minutes until soft.

3   Add the cooked rice, salmon, coriander seeds, cream, hard-boiled eggs and chopped parsley. Season lightly and heat through gently for 2 minutes.

4   Spoon the kedgeree onto warmed serving plates and garnish with the lemon wedges, flat-leaf parsley sprigs and a grinding of black pepper.

TUNA KEDGEREE

This kedgeree can also be made with tuna. Replace the salmon with 213 g canned tuna in sunflower oil – drain and flake the tuna before using.

SALMON WITH A CRUMB CRUST

50 g fine white breadcrumbs

1 tablespoon pine nuts, lightly toasted

4 tablespoons fresh basil, chopped

15 g butter

50 g Parmesan cheese, freshly grated

Salt and pepper, to taste

4 salmon fillets

Serves 4

This recipe is quick and easy and is an ideal dish for a quick midweek supper party – serve with new potatoes and green beans.

1   Heat the grill. Place the breadcrumbs, pine nuts, basil, butter, Parmesan cheese and seasoning in a food processor and blend until combined.

2   Place the salmon under a moderately hot grill for 5 minutes. Turn over, top with the breadcrumb mixture, pressing it down gently with the palm of your hand. Grill for a further 5 minutes, or until the salmon is cooked through.

COD & BROCCOLI CHEESE PIE

*Here, chunks of fish are cooked in a creamy cheese sauce, under a layer
of golden cheese and mashed potato. Mascarpone cheese is a quick way
to make a cheese sauce and is a good source of calcium.*

750 g cod fillet
600 ml full-fat milk
½ onion, sliced
1 carrot, thinly sliced
1 bay leaf
1 kg floury potatoes, such as Maris Piper, peeled and cut into even-sized pieces
75 g butter
150 ml single cream
Salt and pepper, to taste
100 g mature Cheddar cheese, grated
225 g small broccoli florets
1 large leek, thinly sliced
500 g mascarpone cheese
1 tablespoon fresh dill, chopped, plus extra to garnish
Serves 6

1 Preheat the oven to 180°C, gas mark 4. Place the cod in an ovenproof dish and pour over 450 ml of the milk. Add the onion, carrot and the bay leaf. Cover and cook in the oven for 20 minutes. Strain off, and discard, the milk.

2 Meanwhile, cook the potatoes in boiling water for 20 minutes. Drain and return to the saucepan. Add 25 g of the butter and mash smoothly. Add the cream and the remaining milk and beat until light and fluffy. Season well, then fold in half the Cheddar cheese.

3 In the meantime, blanch the broccoli in boiling salted water for 1 minute. Drain well and rinse under cold running water. Set aside on a plate lined with kitchen paper.

4 Melt 25 g of the butter in a saucepan and cook the leeks for 5–7 minutes, until softened. Add the mascarpone and stir well until smooth. Cook for 5–7 minutes until thickened. Stir the chopped dill into the mascarpone and season well.

5 Turn the oven up to 230°C, gas mark 8. Flake the cod in the ovenproof dish, place the broccoli evenly over the flaked fish, then pour over the sauce. Spoon over the mashed potato, covering the filling completely, and sprinkle over the remaining Cheddar cheese. Dot with the remaining butter and bake in the oven for 10–15 minutes until brown on top. Serve garnished with sprigs of fresh dill.

SALMON & BROCCOLI CHEESE PIE
Replace the fresh cod with 750 g fresh salmon fillet. Flavour the mashed potato with some finely chopped spring onions or chopped fresh herbs, such as dill, tarragon or chervil.

PARSNIP TOPPING
Replace half of the potatoes with parsnips to make a parsnip mash topping, then follow the recipe as above.

CARROT TOPPING
For a potato and carrot topping, use 750 g potato and fold 225 g grated carrot into the mash, then follow the recipe as above.

COD BAKED IN YOGURT

150 ml natural yogurt

1 clove garlic, peeled and finely chopped

2.5 cm piece fresh root ginger, peeled and finely chopped

½ teaspoon ground cumin

½ teaspoon ground coriander

¼ teaspoon chilli powder

¼ teaspoon salt

4 skinless cod fillets

Serves 4

This dish is low in fat, making it a good choice for anyone on a weight-reducing or low-fat diet. If you haven't got the individual spices to hand, you could use 1 tablespoon of curry paste instead.
Serve the fish with a tomato salad and naan bread.

1 Mix together the yogurt, garlic, ginger, cumin, coriander, chilli and salt.

2 Place the fish in a shallow dish and pour over the spiced yogurt mixture. Cover and refrigerate for 2–3 hours.

3 Heat the grill. Transfer the fish onto a foil-lined grill pan and cook under a hot grill for 5–8 minutes, or until the fish is cooked through.

POACHED HADDOCK WITH SPINACH & POACHED EGG

2 smoked haddock fillets, about 150 g each

150 ml full-fat milk

2 large eggs

225 g baby spinach leaves, washed and drained

Salt and pepper, to taste

Serves 2

This dish makes a healthy and nutritious lunch or light supper. Spinach provides useful amounts of calcium, particularly for people who don't eat dairy products. Egg yolks are rich in vitamin K which is essential for bone health.

1 Place the haddock in a large shallow pan and pour over the milk. Cover and simmer gently for about 8 minutes, or until cooked through.

2 Meanwhile, bring a pan of water to the boil, then carefully crack the eggs into the water and poach for 2–3 minutes. Remove with a slotted spoon, allowing the water to drain thoroughly. Set aside on plate lined with kitchen paper.

3 Cook the spinach in a large saucepan for 2–3 minutes until just wilted – there is no need to add extra water as enough clings to the leaves after washing. Drain, and season well.

4 Divide the spinach between two plates and place a fillet of haddock upon each. Top each with a poached egg.

FISH PIE WITH ROSTI TOPPING

A crisp potato and red onion topping hides a rich creamy mixture of smoked haddock, petits pois and French beans.

1 Cook the potatoes, whole, in their skins, in plenty of boiling salted water for 15 minutes. Drain well and set aside to cool.

2 Meanwhile, heat the oil in a saucepan and cook the onion for 5–7 minutes, until soft and lightly golden. Peel and coarsely grate the potatoes into a sieve, squeezing out any excess moisture. Mix the potatoes, onion and chopped herbs together and season well. Set aside.

3 Put the haddock, peppercorns and stock in a large pan. Bring to the boil, then cover and simmer gently for about 5–7 minutes, or until the fish is just tender. Remove the fish from the stock and flake the flesh, discarding the skin and any bones. Set aside.

4 Cook the petits pois and French beans in boiling salted water for 4–5 minutes, or until just tender. Drain well.

5 Heat the oven to 200°C, gas mark 6. In a saucepan, gently heat the mascarpone and cook for 5–7 minutes until it has thickened. Put the fish, petits pois and French beans in a shallow ovenproof dish and pour over the cheese sauce. Gently mix and season to taste.

6 Mix the potato and onion with the melted butter and spoon over the fish mixture, making sure it covers the filling. Cook in the oven for 20–25 minutes, until golden brown.

FOR THE TOPPING

750 g large waxy potatoes

2 tablespoons olive oil

1 large red onion, thinly sliced

1 tablespoon fresh mixed herbs, chopped

Salt and pepper, to taste

FOR THE FILLING

450 g smoked haddock fillet

6 whole peppercorns

200 ml fish or vegetable stock

125 g frozen petits pois

125 g French beans, halved

500 g mascarpone cheese

Salt and pepper, to taste

25 g melted butter

Serves 6

DEEP-FRIED WHITEBAIT

Like all fish that are eaten with their bones, whitebait are an excellent source of calcium. Mixing a little plain yogurt with the mayonnaise helps to reduce the fat content and boost the calcium content.

1 Mix the paprika with the flour and season to taste. Toss the whitebait in the seasoned flour.

2 Heat the oil in a deep fat fryer to 190°C. Add the whitebait to the hot oil in batches, cooking each batch for about 3 minutes, until the fish is golden brown. Drain on absorbent kitchen paper and keep warm while you cook the rest.

3 Mix the mayonnaise, yogurt, chives and lemon zest together. Garnish the whitebait with lemon wedges and serve with the yogurt dip.

1 tablespoon paprika

6 tablespoons plain flour

Salt and pepper, to taste

450 g whitebait

Oil, for deep-frying

5 tablespoons mayonnaise

3 tablespoons plain yogurt

2 tablespoon fresh chives, chopped

Zest of 1 lemon

Lemon wedges, to garnish

Serves 4

MONKFISH KEBABS WITH ROASTED VEGETABLES & PESTO

FOR THE ROASTED VEGETABLES

2 red peppers, deseeded and cut into bite-sized pieces

I large aubergine, cut into bite-sized pieces

2 small red onions, peeled and cut into quarters

2 large courgettes, sliced into bite-sized pieces

6 cloves garlic, peeled

4 tablespoons olive oil

Salt and pepper, to taste

FOR THE PESTO

85 g fresh watercress, chopped

I clove garlic, peeled

50 g Parmesan cheese, freshly grated

6 tablespoons olive oil

FOR THE KEBABS

450 g monkfish, cut into 24 bite-sized pieces

6 slices Parma ham, cut into strips

16 cherry tomatoes

Serves 4

Using watercress instead of basil in the pesto helps to boost the calcium content. Watercress is also rich in vitamin C and betacarotene, and provides useful amounts of iron.

1 Preheat the oven to 220°C, gas mark 7. Place the peppers, aubergine, onions, courgettes and garlic in a large roasting tin, drizzle over the olive oil and mix well. Season and place in the oven for 20–30 minutes, until the vegetables are tender.

2 To make the pesto, place the watercress, garlic, Parmesan cheese and olive oil in a blender or food processor and blend until smooth.

3 Wrap each piece of monkfish in a strip of Parma ham. Thread 3 pieces onto each of 8 wood skewers, alternating with cherry tomatoes. (The skewers should be soaked in water for 30 minutes beforehand to prevent burning.)

4 Brush the kebabs with a little oil and place under a hot grill for 3–4 minutes. Turn and cook for a further 3 minutes until cooked through. Serve the kebabs with the roasted vegetables and pesto.

GRIDDLED SWORDFISH WITH SALSA VERDE

Salsa verde is a fresh, tasty sauce, which works particularly well with white fish. Serve this dish with a simple tomato salad. Anchovies are a useful source of calcium particularly for people who don't eat dairy products.

1   To make the salsa verde, place the anchovies, capers and garlic in a food processor and blend for 30 seconds. Add the mint, basil, parsley, mustard, lemon juice and olive oil and blend until smooth.

2   Brush a griddle pan with a little olive oil and heat. When the pan is hot, add the swordfish steaks and cook for 4–5 minutes. Turn and cook for a further 4–5 minutes. Serve with the salsa verde.

4 anchovy fillets, drained and roughly chopped

1 tablespoon capers, drained and rinsed

1 clove garlic, peeled

15 g fresh mint leaves

15 g fresh basil leaves

15 g fresh flat-leaf parsley leaves or 30 g watercress

1 teaspoon Dijon mustard

Juice of 1 lemon

6 tablespoons olive oil, plus extra for brushing

4 swordfish steaks

Serves 4

PRAWN & SPINACH ROULADE

This attractive roulade makes a great summer meal. Make sure the spinach is drained thoroughly before adding it to the sauce.

50 g butter, plus extra for greasing

125 g frozen chopped spinach, thawed and drained

50 g plain flour

300 ml full-fat milk

2 eggs, separated

FOR THE FILLING

250 g mascarpone cheese

4 spring onions, finely chopped

2 sun-dried tomatoes, finely chopped

225 g peeled prawns, cooked

Salt and pepper, to taste

Serves 6

1. Grease and line a 33 × 23 cm Swiss roll tin with non-stick baking parchment. Preheat the oven to 220°C, gas mark 7.

2. Melt the butter in a saucepan and stir in the spinach and flour. Cook for 1 minute, then add the milk. Bring to the boil, stirring continuously, then simmer for 2–3 minutes. Remove from the heat and beat in the egg yolks. In a clean bowl, stiffly whisk the egg whites, then fold into the mixture.

3. Spoon the mixture into the tin and spread out evenly with a palate knife. Bake in the oven for about 15 minutes, or until well-risen and firm to the touch. Turn out on to a sheet of non-stick baking parchment and peel off the lining paper. Leave covered with a damp cloth for 20 minutes to cool.

4. Meanwhile, mix together the mascarpone cheese, spring onions, sun-dried tomatoes and prawns. Season well, then cover until the roulade is cool.

5. Spread the roulade with the prawn filling, leaving a 2.5 cm border. Starting at one long side, gently roll up the roulade, using the paper to help. Serve in thick slices with a crisp green salad.

PENNE WITH PRAWNS & ASPARAGUS

The lemon in this pasta enhances the flavours of the asparagus and the prawns and makes this a light, refreshing dish.

150 g penne or other pasta

125 g asparagus tips

4 tablespoons olive oil

3 tablespoons Parmesan cheese, freshly grated

Zest and juice of 1 large lemon

2 tablespoons fresh chives, snipped

200 g peeled prawns, cooked

Serves 2

1. Cook the pasta according to the manufacturer's instructions. About 4–5 minutes before it has finished cooking, add the asparagus and continue to cook until the asparagus is tender. Drain well and return to the pan.

2. Meanwhile, whisk together the olive oil, Parmesan cheese, lemon zest and juice and chives.

3. Stir in the lemon dressing and prawns. Cook, stirring continuously, for 4–5 minutes, or until the prawns are hot.

WARM LENTIL & FETA SALAD

225 g puy lentils

1 clove garlic, peeled

1 bay leaf

4 tablespoons olive oil

2 tablespoons balsamic vinegar

1 clove garlic, crushed

½ teaspoon salt

½ teaspoon English mustard powder

300 g cherry tomatoes, sliced in half

3 tablespoons fresh parsley, chopped

200 g feta cheese, crumbled

Salt and pepper, to taste

Serves 4

The subtle flavour of the puy lentils is perfectly complemented by the cool feta cheese, which is also a good source of calcium.

1   Place the lentils, garlic and bay leaf in a saucepan. Cover with plenty of water and cook for 30–40 minutes, or until the lentils are just soft.

2   Whisk the olive oil, balsamic vinegar, garlic, salt and mustard powder together in a small bowl, to make a dressing.

3   Drain the lentils and transfer to a warm serving dish. Stir in the tomatoes, parsley and dressing. Add the feta cheese, season to taste and serve.

SPICED SPINACH, LENTIL & FETA FILO PIE

When working with filo it is essential to keep the sheets covered with a damp cloth as you work to prevent them drying out and becoming brittle.

1 Preheat the oven to 190°C, gas mark 5. Lightly grease a 22.5 cm springform tin and set aside.

2 To make the filling, heat the oil in a saucepan. Add the onion, garlic, ground coriander and cumin and fry gently for 10 minutes. Stir in the lentils, cover and heat through for 4–5 minutes, then mash with a fork. Transfer to a bowl and leave to cool slightly.

3 Meanwhile, cook the spinach in a large saucepan for 2–3 minutes until just wilted – there is no need to add extra water as enough clings to the leaves after washing. Refresh under cold running water. Squeeze out any excess water, shred the leaves and add to the bowl with the spiced lentils.

4 Stir the eggs into the mixture, then add the feta, Parmesan cheese, fresh coriander and season to taste. Toss to mix, then set aside.

5 Lay the filo pastry in the base of the prepared tin and brush with a little of the butter. Make sure the filo forms a solid base, but leave plenty overhanging the edges of the tin. Spoon in the filling and fold over the filo to cover the topping completely.

6 Gently scrunch the remaining sheets of filo and arrange on top of the pie to give a ruffled effect. Brush with the remaining butter. Bake for 30–35 minutes until golden. Allow to cool slightly before turning out. Cut into wedges and serve.

---

3 tablespoons olive oil, plus extra for greasing

1 medium red onion, finely chopped

3 garlic cloves, crushed

2 teaspoons ground coriander

1 teaspoon ground cumin

2 x 300 g can lentils, drained

350 g baby spinach leaves, washed

2 eggs, beaten

175 g feta cheese, crumbled

2 tablespoons Parmesan cheese, freshly grated

4 tablespoons fresh coriander, chopped

Salt and pepper, to taste

12 sheets of filo pastry (or 6 large sheets, halved)

75 g unsalted butter, melted

Serves 6

CHEESE & LEEK SAUSAGES

175 g fine white breadcrumbs

125 g Caerphilly or Cheddar cheese

1 small leek, trimmed and finely chopped

1 tablespoon fresh parsley, finely chopped

Pinch of mustard powder

Salt and pepper, to taste

1 egg, beaten

2–3 tablespoons milk

Plain flour, for coating

Vegetable oil, for frying or brushing

Serves 4

These are ideal for children, but adults are sure to love them, too. They provide a good alternative to meat-filled sausages.

1 In a large bowl, mix together the breadcrumbs, cheese, leek, parsley and mustard powder. Season to taste. Add the egg and mix thoroughly, then add enough milk to bind the mixture together.

2 Divide the mixture into 8 and shape into sausages.

3 If shallow frying, roll the sausages in the flour. Heat a little oil in a large non-stick frying pan, add the sausages and fry for about 5 minutes, or until golden brown. Alternatively, lightly brush the sausages with a little oil and cook under a hot grill for about 3–4 minutes, turning occasionally. Serve hot or cold.

VEGETABLE PATTIES

350 g potatoes, peeled and cut into even-sized pieces

3 tablespoons semi-skimmed milk

350 g mixed vegetables

3 tablespoons vegetable oil

1 small onion, finely chopped

1 clove garlic, crushed

200 g Cheddar cheese, grated

Salt and pepper, to taste

25 g plain flour, for dusting

1 egg, beaten

125 g fine white breadcrumbs

Serves 4

You can use any mixed vegetables you like in these patties, such as carrots, broccoli, spinach, peas and sweetcorn. They are delicious served with a tomato salad.

1 Cook the potatoes in boiling, salted water for 15–20 minutes. Drain well, then mash with the milk. Steam the mixed vegetables and chop finely.

2 Heat 1 tablespoon of the oil in a large non-stick frying pan. Add the onion and garlic and cook over a medium heat for 5 minutes until soft.

3 Stir the cooked vegetables, onion and garlic mixture and the grated cheese into the mashed potato. Season to taste, cover and chill for 1 hour.

4 Turn the mixture onto a floured surface and shape into 8 rounds. Dip the patties into the beaten egg and coat in the breadcrumbs. Chill for 15 minutes.

5 Heat the remaining oil and fry the patties, in batches, over a medium heat for 3–4 minutes on each side, or until golden brown.

BUBBLE & SQUEAK

The vegetable mixture also makes a delicious bubble and squeak. Follow the recipe up until the end of step 3. Heat 1 tablespoon of oil in a large non-stick frying pan, add the mixture and fry until heated through and browned.

SPICED TOFU BURGERS

Using tofu for these vegetarian burgers ensures that they are lower in fat than those that contain a large quantity of nuts. Serve in a burger bun with mayonnaise, lettuce and slices of tomato, not forgetting the oven chips.

1 Heat the oil in a large non-stick frying pan. Add the carrots and onion and cook, stirring continuously, for 3–4 minutes, or until the vegetables are soft. Add the ground coriander, garlic, curry paste and tomato purée. Increase the heat and cook for 2 minutes, stirring all the time.

2 Mash the tofu with a potato masher, then stir into the vegetables along with the breadcrumbs and nuts. Season well and stir until the mixture starts to stick together.

3 With floured hands, shape the mixture into 4 burgers. Heat a little of the oil in a large non-stick frying pan and fry the burgers for 3–4 minutes on each side, or until golden brown. Alternatively, to grill the burgers, brush them with a little oil and cook under a preheated grill for about 3 minutes on each side. Drain on kitchen paper and serve.

I tablespoon vegetable oil

I large carrot, grated

I large red onion, grated

2 teaspoons ground coriander

I garlic clove, peeled and crushed

I teaspoon hot curry paste

I teaspoon sun-dried tomato purée

225 g tofu, drained

25 g wholemeal breadcrumbs

25 g mixed nuts, toasted and finely chopped

Salt and pepper, to taste

Plain flour, for dusting

Vegetable oil, for frying or grilling

Makes 4 burgers

ROASTED THAI-STYLE TOFU WITH STIR-FRIED VEGETABLES

450 g tofu, drained

I garlic clove, peeled and finely chopped

2 tablespoons hoisin sauce

2 tablespoons dark soy sauce

I tablespoon sherry vinegar

I tablespoon sweet chilli sauce

I tablespoon runny honey

I teaspoon sesame oil

FOR THE STIR-FRY

3 tablespoons sunflower oil

I teaspoon sesame oil

I medium red onion, roughly chopped

2 carrots, cut into matchsticks

I red pepper, thinly sliced

175 g broccoli florets

125 g chestnut mushrooms, quartered

6 spring onions, sliced

125 g sugar snap peas

Toasted sesame seeds, to garnish

Serves 4

Tofu is ideal for the modern healthy diet because it is low in fat and is a good source of protein. Here, the tofu is glazed in a Thai-style sauce and served with a selection of stir-fried vegetables. Egg noodles or plain boiled rice make ideal accompaniments.

1 Preheat the oven to 220°C, gas mark 8. Cut the tofu into 2.5 cm cubes and place in a shallow roasting tin. Mix together the garlic, hoisin sauce, soy sauce, sherry vinegar, chilli sauce, honey and sesame oil. Pour two-thirds of the marinade over the tofu and toss well, making sure the tofu is coated thoroughly. Roast for 25 minutes, turning once, until the tofu is deep golden brown and glazed.

2 Meanwhile, heat both oils in a wok or large non-stick frying pan. Add the red onion, carrots, red pepper, broccoli and mushrooms and stir-fry for 3 minutes. Add the spring onions and sugar snap peas and stir-fry for a further 2 minutes.

3 Add 2 tablespoons of water to the remaining glaze and add this to the stir-fried vegetables. Cook for another 2–3 minutes until the vegetables are just tender, then stir in the roasted tofu. Garnish with toasted sesame seeds and serve immediately.

MARINATED TOFU WITH SATAY SAUCE

Pressed tofu is ideal for marinating because it contains less liquid and will, therefore, absorb more flavour. The satay sauce can be made in advance and reheated before serving.

1 Cut the tofu into 1 cm pieces. In a shallow dish, mix together the onion, soy sauce and sugar. Add the tofu pieces and toss, ensuring that the tofu is thoroughly coated. Cover and leave to marinate for at least 1 hour. Soak 8 wooden skewers in cold water for 30 minutes.

2 Meanwhile, for the satay sauce, heat the oil in a saucepan and add the garlic and chilli powder. Cook, stirring, for 1–2 minutes. Add the peanut butter, sugar and lemon zest, along with 300 ml water. Bring to a simmer and cook for 4–5 minutes until the sauce thickens.

3 Heat the grill to high. Thread the tofu onto 8 skewers. Cook for 3–4 minutes on each side, turning occasionally until browned.

4 Serve on a bed of salad leaves, onions and carrot chunks, accompanied by the satay sauce.

GRILLED VEGETABLES WITH SATAY SAUCE

Grill a selection of vegetables, such as peppers, tomatoes, courgettes, onions or shallots and serve with the satay sauce.

---

250 g pressed tofu

I small onion, finely chopped

3 tablespoons dark soy sauce

I teaspoon dark muscovado sugar

FOR THE SATAY SAUCE

I tablespoon vegetable oil

I clove garlic, peeled and crushed

2 teaspoons chilli powder

225 g crunchy peanut butter

I tablespoon dark muscovado sugar

Zest of I large lemon

TO SERVE

Selection of salad leaves, chopped onion and carrot chunks

Serves 4

HOT SPICED CHICKPEAS

*This dish is delicious warm, accompanied by crusty wholemeal bread,
but can also be served cold with a wild rocket leaf salad.*

1 Heat the oil in a large saucepan and sauté the onions for 5–7 minutes,
until soft.

2 Add the turmeric and cumin seeds and fry for 1 minute, stirring
frequently. Add the chickpeas, tomatoes, lemon juice and coriander and
sauté for 4–5 minutes until heated through.

3 Season well and serve garnished with coriander leaves and a sprinkling
of cayenne pepper.

1 tablespoon vegetable oil

1 large red onion, roughly chopped

2 teaspoons ground turmeric

1 tablespoon cumin seeds

2 x 400 g cans chickpeas, drained
and rinsed

450 g cherry tomatoes, halved

1 tablespoon lemon juice

4 tablespoons fresh coriander, chopped

Salt and pepper, to taste

Fresh coriander leaves, to garnish

Cayenne pepper, to garnish

Serves 6

CHICKPEA & POTATO STEW

*A quick and easy stew using canned chickpeas and potatoes
flavoured with Indian spices. Serve with boiled pilau rice.*

1 In a large saucepan, heat the oil and cook the onion for 5 minutes until soft.

2 Add the garlic and curry paste and cook for 30 seconds, stirring frequently.
Stir in the potato, chickpeas and chilli and season well. Add the stock and
150 ml water. Simmer for 30 minutes.

3 Add the spring onions, 3 tablespoons of chopped coriander, lime juice and
garam masala. Reheat and simmer for 2–3 minutes. Season to taste.
Garnish with the remaining chopped coriander and serve.

CHICKPEA AND SWEET POTATO STEW
For an interesting variation on this recipe, replace the potato with sweet potato
which will give it a more mellow flavour.

2 tablespoons sunflower oil

2 medium red onions, chopped

4 cloves garlic, peeled and chopped

2 tablespoons medium-hot curry paste

450 g potatoes, diced

2 x 400 g cans chickpeas, drained
and rinsed

1 red chilli, deseeded and chopped

Salt and pepper, to taste

300 ml vegetable stock

6 spring onions, chopped

4 tablespoons fresh coriander, chopped

Juice of 1 lime

1 teaspoon garam masala

Serves 4

MIXED BEANS WITH A CORNMEAL TOPPING

FOR THE BEANS

1 tablespoon olive oil

1 small onion, finely chopped

2 garlic cloves, peeled and finely chopped

400 g can chopped tomatoes

200 ml vegetable stock

2 tablespoons dark soy sauce

3 tablespoons dark brown sugar

1 tablespoon mild mustard

2 x 400 g cans of mixed beans, rinsed and drained

FOR THE TOPPING

50 g self-raising flour

50 g cornmeal (polenta)

¼ teaspoon salt

½ teaspoon baking powder

5 tablespoons full-fat milk

2 eggs, separated

1 tablespoon olive oil

125 g Cheddar cheese, grated

Serves 4

Canned beans and pulses are a good store cupboard ingredient. They are rich in soluble fibre (the type that helps reduce cholesterol levels) and are also a useful source of calcium.

1 Heat 1 tablespoon of the oil in a saucepan. Add the onion and garlic and cook for 5 minutes until soft. Add the tomatoes, stock and soy sauce. Bring to the boil, then reduce to a fast simmer and cook for about 15 minutes, or until the sauce begins to thicken.

2 Add the sugar, mustard and mixed beans. Continue to cook for a further 5 minutes, until the beans are hot.

3 Preheat the oven to 200°C, gas mark 6. Meanwhile, make the topping; mix the flour, cornmeal, salt, baking powder, milk, egg yolks, oil and 75 g of the cheese in a bowl. Beat together to make a fairly stiff batter, adding a little extra milk if necessary.

4 Whisk the egg whites in a clean bowl until stiff, then, using a metal spoon, fold carefully into the batter.

5 Transfer the beans to a shallow ovenproof dish and spoon over the topping. Sprinkle over the remaining Cheddar cheese and cook for 20 minutes, until the topping is golden brown and well risen.

BUTTERNUT SQUASH & GRUYERE RISOTTO

You can use any type of squash or pumpkin to make this delicious creamy risotto. The secret of a good risotto is to keep it simmering slowly while you add the stock a little at a time, so it cooks evenly. Arborio rice is the best-known Italian rice and is ideal for risotto – its plump, long grains absorb liquid without losing their bite.

1 Heat the oil in a large saucepan, add the leeks, garlic, chilli, rosemary and sage and cook for 5 minutes until soft.

2 Add the rice and stir-fry for 1 minute until all the grains are glossy. Bring the vegetable stock to a steady simmer in another saucepan.

3 Add the butternut squash and stir well. Pour in 150 ml of the hot stock and stir over a medium heat until absorbed. Gradually add the remaining stock, a ladleful at a time, stirring occasionally, making sure each addition is absorbed before adding the next. Continue until the rice is tender and all the stock absorbed – this should take about 25 minutes.

4 Remove from the heat and stir in 100 g of the Gruyère cheese and the cream. Cover and allow to stand for 5 minutes. Season well to taste.

5 Top with the remaining 25 g of the Gruyère cheese and a grinding of black pepper. Garnish with small fresh rosemary sprigs and Gruyère shavings.

4 tablespoons extra virgin olive oil

2 leeks, trimmed and thinly sliced

2 garlic cloves, finely chopped

I red chilli, deseeded and thinly sliced

I tablespoon fresh rosemary, chopped

I tablespoon fresh sage, chopped

225 g arborio rice

I litre vegetable stock

450 g butternut squash, peeled, deseeded and chopped

125 g Gruyère cheese, grated

4 tablespoons double cream

Salt and pepper, to taste

Small fresh rosemary sprigs, to garnish

Gruyère shavings, to garnish

Serves 4

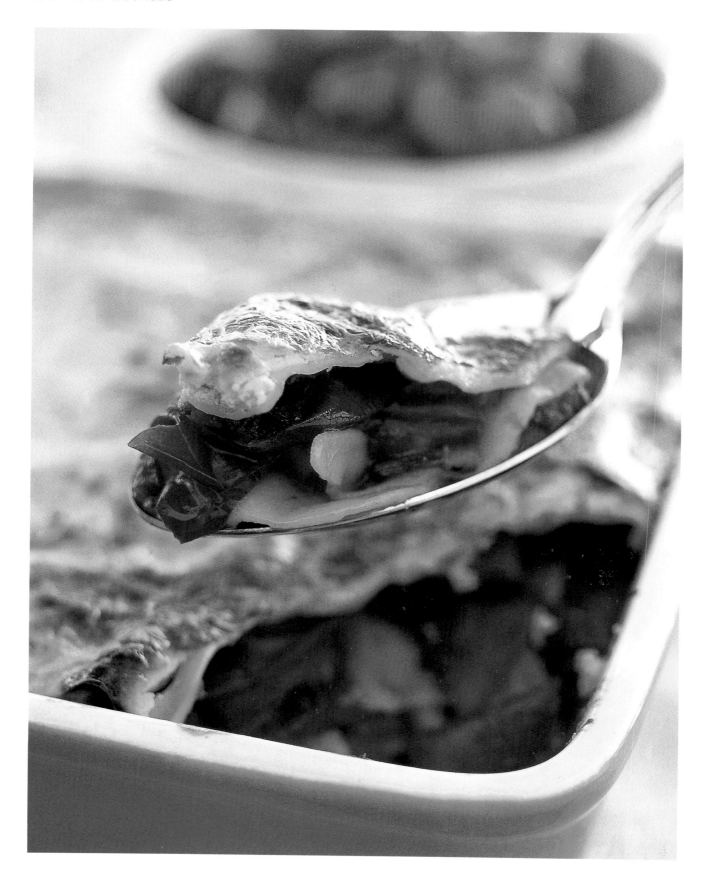

ROASTED VEGETABLE LASAGNE

Served with a tomato and basil salad, this recipe provides a healthy, balanced meal. You can use pre-cooked lasagne sheets, but add a little extra liquid to the vegetable and tomato mixture.

1 Preheat the oven to 190°C, gas mark 5. Place the chopped vegetables in a large shallow roasting tin. Toss in the oil and season well. Roast for 25–30 minutes until slightly blackened. Leave to cool slightly.

2 Meanwhile, mix together the ricotta cheese with the egg, milk and 4 tablespoons of the Parmesan cheese. Season well and set aside.

3 Spoon the roasted vegetables into a large bowl and mix with the canned tomatoes (use those with added garlic and herbs for extra flavour) and basil. Spoon a layer of vegetable and tomato mixture over the base of a lightly greased ovenproof dish and cover with a layer of lasagne sheets.

4 Continue with another layer of the vegetable and tomato mixture, then another layer of lasagne. Repeat this process once more, then spread the ricotta cheese mixture evenly over the top and sprinkle with the remaining Parmesan cheese. Bake for 30 minutes or until golden brown and bubbling.

5 Leave the lasagne to stand for 5 minutes before serving.

1 large courgette, roughly chopped

1 red pepper, deseeded and chopped

1 red onion, roughly chopped

1 small aubergine, chopped

2 tablespoons olive oil

Salt and pepper, to taste

250 g ricotta cheese

1 egg

4 tablespoons full-fat milk

6 tablespoons Parmesan cheese, grated

2 x 400 g cans chopped tomatoes

2 tablespoons fresh basil, chopped

8–10 sheets fresh lasagne

Serves 4

PAPPARDELLE WITH SPICY TOMATO SAUCE & RICOTTA

Ricotta cheese is surprisingly low in fat compared with many other cheeses, but still provides useful amounts of calcium. The creaminess of the ricotta perfectly balances the heat of the sauce. If time is short, use ready-made arrabbiata sauce instead of making your own tomato sauce.

1 Heat the oil in large saucepan, add the onion, garlic, ground coriander and cumin and cook for 5 minutes, or until the onions are soft. Add the tomatoes, tomato purée, red wine and seasoning, bring to the boil, then simmer for about 30 minutes, or until the sauce has reduced by about half.

2 Cook the pasta according to the packet instructions and drain well.

3 Transfer the pasta to a serving dish, spoon over the tomato sauce, then stir in the ricotta cheese. Garnish with fresh basil and serve immediately.

1 tablespoon olive oil

1 large red onion, finely chopped

1 clove garlic, peeled and finely chopped

1 teaspoon ground coriander

1 teaspoon ground cumin

2 x 400 g cans chopped tomatoes

1 tablespoon tomato purée

150 ml red wine

Salt and pepper, to taste

250 g pappardelle, or other pasta

200 g ricotta cheese

Fresh basil, chopped, to garnish

Serves 4

BROCCOLI & GRUYERE SOUFFLE

Broccoli is good source of vitamin K, which is an important nutrient for bone health. It also provides useful amounts of calcium, so is particularly good for people on a dairy-free diet.

1 Preheat the oven to 180°C, gas mark 4. Grease 6 ramekin dishes and place on a baking tray. Steam the broccoli over a pan of boiling water for 8 minutes until tender.

2 Melt the butter in a saucepan, stir in the flour and cook for 1 minute. Gradually stir in the milk and bring to the boil. Cook, stirring continuously, until the mixture has thickened.

3 Pour the sauce into a food processor, add the broccoli and purée until the mixture is smooth.

4 Transfer the mixture to a bowl, allow to cool slightly, then stir in the egg yolks and Gruyère cheese. Season to taste.

5 In a clean bowl, whisk the egg whites until stiff, then lightly fold into the sauce mixture.

6 Spoon into the ramekin dishes, transfer to the oven and cook for 20–25 minutes, or until the soufflés are just firm to the touch. Serve immediately.

Butter, for greasing

225 g broccoli florets

40 g butter

3 tablespoons plain flour

200 ml full-fat milk

3 eggs, separated

125 g Gruyère cheese, grated

Salt and pepper, to taste

Serves 6

SPINACH AND GRUYERE SOUFFLE

Replace the broccoli with 225 g cooked spinach. Squeeze any excess moisture from the spinach and follow the instructions above.

MEDITERRANEAN STUFFED PEPPERS WITH COUSCOUS

Couscous is an ideal accompaniment to these tasty and healthy stuffed peppers. They can also be served on top of toasted ciabatta rubbed with garlic, accompanied by a rocket salad.

1 Preheat the oven to 180°C, gas mark 4. Cut the peppers in half through the stalks. Scoop out the seeds and the white ribs, leaving the stalk intact. Put the pepper halves cut-side up into a large roasting tin and set aside.

2 To remove the tomato skins, mark a cross in the top of each one and put them into a bowl. Cover with boiling water and leave for 1 minute, then drain. Leave to cool slightly then peel off the skin and cut the tomatoes into wedges.

3 Mix the tomato wedges, garlic, capers, olives and oregano together, then spoon into the pepper halves. Drizzle over the olive oil and season well.

4 Roast for 35 minutes. Remove from the oven and scatter over the feta and pine nuts or shredded almonds. Return to the oven and cook for a further 10 minutes, or until the feta has melted and the nuts are lightly golden.

5 Meanwhile, put the couscous into a large bowl and pour over the boiling water or vegetable stock. Leave for about 5 minutes until the stock is absorbed and the couscous soft. Fluff up the couscous mixture with a fork and toss in the chopped parsley, spring onions, lemon zest and a drizzle of olive oil.

6 To serve, place a little couscous and 2 roasted pepper halves onto each of 4 serving plates. Garnish with parsley and a grinding of black pepper.

FOR THE STUFFED PEPPERS

4 large red peppers

12 cherry tomatoes, halved

3 cloves garlic, peeled and thinly sliced

1 teaspoon capers, drained and rinsed

8 pitted black olives, roughly chopped

1 tablespoon fresh oregano, chopped

4 tablespoons virgin olive oil

Salt and pepper, to taste

125 g feta cheese, crumbled

2 tablespoons pine nuts or shredded almonds

FOR THE COUSCOUS

225 g couscous

300 ml boiling water or hot vegetable stock

2 tablespoons fresh flat-leaf parsley, chopped, plus extra to garnish

4 spring onions, shredded

Zest of 1 lemon

Olive oil, for drizzling

Serves 4

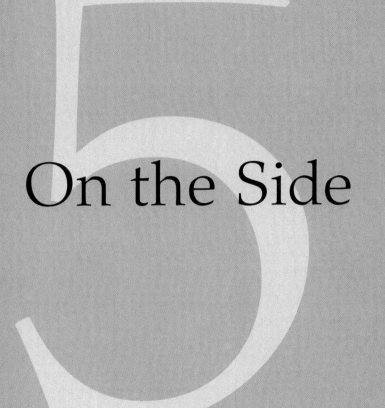

On the Side

ACCOMPANIMENTS CAN SOMETIMES
BECOME A SECOND THOUGHT WHEN
PREPARING A MEAL, SO THIS CHAPTER
OFFERS CREATIVE IDEAS FOR
VEGETABLE SIDE DISHES AND SALADS
THAT WILL BOOST THE FLAVOUR AND
NUTRITIONAL VALUE OF ANY DISH.

FRENCH BEANS WITH FETA & SUN-DRIED TOMATOES

250 g green beans, trimmed

75 g feta cheese, crumbled

50 g sun-dried tomatoes in oil, sliced into thin strips

Salt and pepper, to taste

Serves 4

The combination of feta and sun-dried tomatoes gives this accompaniment a classic Mediterranean flavour. It works well with plain grilled meat or fish.

1 Cook the beans in a large pan of boiling salted water for 3–4 minutes or until just tender. Drain well.

2 Toss the beans with the feta cheese and sun-dried tomatoes. Season to taste and serve.

ROASTED BABY CARROTS WITH PARMESAN & CORIANDER TOPPING

600 g baby carrots

1 tablespoon sunflower oil

1 tablespoon unsalted butter

Salt and pepper, to taste

3 tablespoons fresh coriander, chopped

50 g Parmesan cheese, freshly grated

Serves 4

The Parmesan cheese and coriander topping is quick and tasty and works well with most vegetables. Adding a cheesy crust is also a great way to persuade kids to eat vegetables.

1 Preheat the oven to 200°C, gas mark 6. Put the carrots in a large saucepan of boiling water and boil for 3 minutes. Drain well.

2 Place the carrots in a shallow ovenproof dish with the oil, butter and seasoning. Roast in the oven for 15 minutes.

3 Meanwhile, mix the coriander and Parmesan cheese together in a small bowl. Remove the carrots from the oven and sprinkle with the mixture. Return to the oven for another 10 minutes, until the carrots are tender and lightly golden.

SPICY ROAST BABY CARROTS WITH FETA
Follow steps 1 and 2 as above. With a pestle and mortar, grind together 1 teaspoon coriander seeds, 1 teaspoon ground cardamom, 1 bay leaf, 1 teaspoon cumin seeds, 6 peppercorns, 1 teaspoon hot paprika and half a cinnamon stick. Sprinkle this mixture over the roasted carrots and toss lightly, then crumble over 200 g feta cheese. Return the carrots to the oven for 10 minutes until they are tender and the cheese has melted.

ASIAN-STYLE BROCCOLI

*Lightly steamed broccoli is a useful source of calcium. It also
provides good amounts of betacarotene, vitamin C,
vitamin B$_6$, folate and niacin.*

1 Cook the broccoli in a large pan of boiling salted water for 1–2 minutes.
Immediately plunge the broccoli into ice-cold water to stop it cooking
further. Drain well and blot dry with absorbent kitchen paper.

2 Heat the sesame and sunflower oils in a wok or large frying pan. Add the
garlic, chilli and ginger and stir-fry for 2–3 minutes. Add the broccoli and
soy sauce and continue to cook for 1 minute. Sprinkle with the sesame
seeds and serve.

450 g broccoli, divided into small florets

2 teaspoons sesame oil

2 teaspoons sunflower oil

1 clove garlic, peeled and finely chopped

1 red chilli, deseeded and finely chopped

1 cm fresh ginger, chopped

1 tablespoon light soy sauce

1 teaspoon sesame seeds

Serves 4

HONEYED PARSNIPS WITH SESAME SEEDS

700 g parsnips, peeled

50 g butter

2 tablespoons honey

2 tablespoons sesame seeds, toasted

Salt and pepper, to taste

Fresh thyme sprigs, to garnish

Serves 4

Sesame seeds are a good source of calcium, particularly for anyone following a dairy-free diet. One tablespoon of sesame seeds will provide around 10 per cent of the daily calcium requirement for women aged between 19 and 50. It also provides around 10 per cent of the daily iron requirement and 17 per cent of the daily vitamin B_6 requirement.

1 Cut the parsnips in half lengthways and in half again. (If using older, tougher parsnips, cut into quarters and remove the woody cores.) Add the parsnips to a pan of boiling salted water and cook for 5 minutes.

2 Meanwhile, melt the butter in a large saucepan. Add the honey and heat gently, stirring until it is dissolved.

3 Drain the parsnips, then add the honey mixture to the pan and toss well to coat the parsnips. Cook over a moderate heat for about 10 minutes, shaking the pan frequently, until the parsnips are golden brown. Sprinkle over the sesame seeds and toss through. Season to taste.

4 Transfer to a warmed serving dish and garnish with thyme sprigs.

PARSNIPS WITH A SWEET LIME GLAZE

Prepare the parsnips as in step 1. Remove the zest from 1 lime and reserve. Put the juice of the lime, 50 g butter and 25 g soft light brown sugar in a large pan and heat until the butter is melted and the sugar dissolved. Follow the recipe as above, using the sweet lime butter in place of the honey mixture. At the end of cooking, stir through 75 g walnuts instead of the sesame seeds. Garnish with the lime zest and fresh thyme sprigs. This sweet lime glaze can be used with any sweet root vegetables, such as sweet potatoes or carrots.

FANTAIL ROAST POTATOES WITH SESAME SEEDS

A roast dinner wouldn't be the same without roast potatoes, and these look attractive as well as tasting great. The sesame seeds give them a crunchy, slightly nutty taste and boost the calcium content of the dish. They are also an ideal source of potassium, which is an important ingredient for healthy bones.

1.8 kg potatoes, peeled and cut into large even-sized pieces

Salt and pepper, to taste

Vegetable oil, for basting

2 tablespoons sesame seeds

Fresh parsley sprigs, to garnish

Serves 6

1   Preheat the oven to 180°C, gas mark 4. Place the potatoes in a large saucepan, cover with salted cold water and bring to the boil, then cook for 3 minutes. Drain well and rinse under cold running water to cool slightly.

2   Using a sharp knife, slice into each potato at 3–5 mm intervals, cutting ¾ of the way through.

3   Heat a thin layer of oil in a large roasting tin in the oven. Add the potatoes and turn over in the oil to coat. Place cut-side up and sprinkle with the sesame seeds.

4   Roast the potatoes for about 1–1¼ hours, basting occasionally. Increase the oven temperature to 220°C, gas mark 7 and roast for a further 15 minutes, until the outside of the potatoes is crisp and golden brown. Serve garnished with parsley sprigs.

RED PESTO FANTAIL ROAST POTATOES

Follow the main recipe as above, omitting the sesame seeds. After the potatoes have been roasting for 1–1¼ hours, remove from the oven. Carefully pull the potatoes apart and spread a little red pesto between each slice – use about 3 tablespoons of pesto altogether. Close the potatoes back up and baste the tops with a little oil from the roasting tin. Increase the oven temperature, as in the main recipe, and roast for a further 15 minutes. Serve with a salad of rocket leaves, crumbled feta, cherry tomatoes, marinated red pepper and a drizzle of olive oil.

Sweet Potato & Anchovy Gratin

450 ml full-fat milk

150 ml double cream

Butter, for greasing

1 kg sweet potatoes, sliced

2 red onions, sliced

50 g canned anchovies, drained and cut in half lengthways

2 cloves garlic, peeled and finely chopped

Salt and pepper, to taste

125 g Gruyère cheese, grated

Serves 6

Sweet potatoes are an excellent source of betacarotene and provide good amounts of vitamin C and potassium, which are important for bone health. This dish is a perfect accompaniment for roast lamb.

1 Put the milk and cream into a saucepan. Bring slowly to the boil, remove from the heat and set aside.

2 Preheat the oven to 200°C, gas mark 6. Grease a 1.8 litre ovenproof dish.

3 Layer the potatoes and onions in the dish with the anchovies, garlic and seasoning between the layers.

4 Pour the warm milk and cream over the potato and onion mixture. Cover the dish with foil, place on a baking sheet and bake for 1 hour. Remove the foil and scatter over the Gruyère cheese. Bake for a further 15–20 minutes until tender and golden. Serve hot.

Aubergine & Tomato Gratin

250 g mascarpone cheese

4 tablespoons Parmesan cheese, freshly grated

Salt and pepper, to taste

2 medium aubergines

Light olive oil or vegetable oil, for frying

6 plum tomatoes, sliced

2 cloves garlic, peeled and roughly chopped

2 eggs, beaten

Fresh thyme leaves, to garnish

Serves 6

This creamy vegetable gratin is an excellent accompaniment to lamb. It also makes a tasty vegetarian main course when served with pasta.

1 Preheat the oven to 200°C, gas mark 6. In a saucepan, heat the mascarpone cheese for 1–2 minutes until smooth. Stir in half the Parmesan cheese and season well. Set aside.

2 Thinly slice the aubergines. Pour enough oil into a large non-stick frying pan to cover the base. Heat until the oil is very hot, then add a layer of aubergine slices – you will need to cook the aubergine in 2 batches. Fry over a moderate heat until golden brown on both sides, turning once. Remove with a slotted spoon and drain on absorbent kitchen paper. Repeat again with the remaining aubergine slices, adding more oil, if necessary.

3 Arrange alternate layers of aubergine and tomato in a greased ovenproof dish. Sprinkle a little garlic, a little salt and plenty of pepper in between each layer.

4 Beat the eggs into the cheese sauce, then slowly pour over the aubergine and tomato. Sprinkle the remaining cheese over the top. Bake for 20 minutes, or until the topping is golden and bubbling. Garnish with thyme leaves and serve hot.

CAULIFLOWER & BROCCOLI CHEESE

Adding a rich, creamy mascarpone sauce to a combination of vegetables transforms this family favourite.

350 g cauliflower florets

350 g broccoli florets

1 teaspoon vegetable oil

4 spring onions, finely shredded

500 g mascarpone cheese

125 g Cheddar cheese, grated

Salt and pepper, to taste

3 tablespoons fresh wholemeal breadcrumbs

Fresh flat-leaf parsley, roughly chopped, to garnish

Serves 6

1 Preheat the oven to 200°C, gas mark 6. Put the cauliflower and broccoli in a pan of boiling salted water. Bring back to the boil and cook for 6–7 minutes until just tender, then drain thoroughly. Place in an ovenproof dish.

2 Heat the oil in a frying pan and stir-fry the spring onions for 2–3 minutes, until softened. Add the mascarpone cheese and cook for 1–2 minutes until smooth. Stir in the half the Cheddar cheese and season well.

3 Pour the cheese sauce evenly over the cauliflower and broccoli. Sprinkle with the breadcrumbs and the remaining cheese and bake for 25 minutes, until the topping is golden and bubbling. Garnish with flat-leaf parsley and a grinding of fresh black pepper.

APPLE, WALNUT & WATERCRESS SALAD

Apples and walnuts are a classic combination and help to give this salad a wonderful crunchy texture. Watercress provides a useful source of calcium, particularly for people on dairy-free diets.

50 g walnut halves

2 teaspoons sherry vinegar

3 tablespoons olive oil

1 tablespoon walnut oil

Salt and pepper, to taste

1 small red onion, peeled and thinly sliced

2 crisp green eating apples, quartered, cored and sliced

100 g watercress

Serves 4

1 To make the salad dressing, chop half the walnuts very finely by hand, or in a food processor. Place in a bowl and whisk in the vinegar, olive oil and walnut oil and season with salt and pepper. Set aside until ready to use.

2 Toss the onion, apple and watercress together in a bowl. Whisk the salad dressing and drizzle it over the salad. Sprinkle with the remaining walnut halves to serve.

POTATO SALAD WITH BLUE CHEESE DRESSING

A high-calcium version of a popular side dish, this is perfect as an accompaniment, and also great for a picnic or buffet lunch.

1   Place the potatoes in a pan of boiling salted water and boil for 15–20 minutes, until cooked through.

2   Whisk together the fromage frais and milk, then stir in the cheese.

3   Drain the potatoes well and place in a serving dish. Cover with the blue cheese dressing and sprinkle with chives. Stir well to ensure the potatoes are coated with the dressing, then serve.

550 g new potatoes, sliced in half

5 tablespoons natural fromage frais

3 tablespoons semi-skimmed milk

125 g Stilton or other blue cheese, crumbled or chopped into small pieces

2 tablespoons fresh chives, chopped

Serves 4

6 Puddings & Treats

Though we don't normally think of desserts as being nutritious, they can provide good quantities of vitamins and minerals. The recipes that follow incorporate carefully chosen, healthy ingredients, and all taste delicious.

Fudgy Nut Pie

225 g ready-made shortcrust pastry

Flour, for dusting

75 g plain chocolate, broken into small pieces

50 g butter

175 g golden caster sugar

75 g soft light brown sugar

100 ml full-fat milk

75 g golden syrup

1 teaspoon vanilla essence

½ teaspoon salt

3 eggs

125 g mixed nuts, chopped

Icing sugar, for dusting

Serves 6

This dessert is deliciously indulgent and is bound to be a hit with the whole family. Serve with vanilla ice cream or crème fraîche.

1. Roll out the pastry on a lightly floured surface and use to line a 23 cm loose-bottomed, 4 cm deep, flan tin. Place on a baking sheet, cover and chill for 30 minutes. Preheat the oven to 200°C, gas mark 6.

2. Prick the pastry with a fork, then line with a large sheet of greaseproof paper and fill with baking beans. Bake for 10–15 minutes, then carefully remove the paper and the beans and return to the oven for a further 5 minutes, until the base is firm to the touch and lightly golden. Remove from the oven and set aside while making the filling.

3. To make the filling, melt the chocolate and butter in a large bowl over hot water. Remove from the heat and add the sugar, milk, golden syrup, vanilla essence, salt and eggs. Beat with a wooden spoon until smooth, then stir in the nuts.

4. Pour the filling into the pastry case and bake at 180°C, gas mark 4 for 45–55 minutes, until puffy and golden. Leave to cool. Dust with icing sugar to serve.

Spiced Apple & Raisin Pancakes

FOR THE FILLING

50 g raisins

3 tablespoons dark rum

900 g Bramley apples, peeled, cored and sliced

5 tablespoons water

3–4 tablespoons caster sugar

Pinch of ground cinnamon

A sweet treat that isn't loaded with fat or calories, these pancakes are delicious served on their own, or with a scoop of vanilla ice cream.

1. To make the filling, place the raisins in a small bowl, pour over the rum and leave to stand for 30 minutes. Place the apples and water in a large pan, cover, and cook gently for about 10 minutes, stirring occasionally. Stir in the sugar, cinnamon and soaked raisins.

2. To make the pancakes, place the flour and salt in a large bowl. Add the egg and half the milk and mix for 1 minute until the mixture is bubbly – use an electric hand mixer if you have one. Stir in the rest of the milk. Pour the batter into a jug and leave to stand for 20 minutes.

3   Heat an 18 cm pancake pan. Add a little oil and, when it starts to smoke, pour in just enough batter to thinly coat the base of the pan. Cook over a moderate heat for about 1 minute or until the bottom is golden brown. Turn the pancake over and cook on the other side for another 30 seconds. Slide the pancake onto a plate, cover with foil, and keep warm in a low oven (150°C, gas mark 2) while you make the rest of the pancakes. Add extra oil to the pan as necessary.

4   Gently reheat the apple mixture. Spoon a little of the mixture into the middle of each pancake and roll. Serve with Greek yogurt.

FOR THE PANCAKES

125 g plain flour, sieved

Pinch of salt

1 large egg

300 ml semi-skimmed milk

Sunflower oil, for frying

Greek yogurt, to serve

Serves 4 (makes 8 pancakes)

RICH CHOCOLATE & FIG PUDDINGS WITH CHOCOLATE SAUCE

The chocolate and figs complement each other perfectly to produce these wonderfully rich, fruity desserts. A generous spoonful of crème fraîche is a good accompaniment.

1   Preheat the oven to 180°C, gas mark 4. Mix the figs and syrup together and divide the mixture between 6 buttered 150 ml dariole moulds.

2   Cream the butter and sugar together until light and fluffy, then beat in the eggs, a little at a time. Sift the flour, baking powder and cocoa powder together and fold into the egg mixture. Stir in the melted chocolate and breadcrumbs.

3   Spoon the mixture into the dariole moulds until they are two-thirds full. Cover with foil and place in a roasting tin containing enough hot water to come half-way up the moulds. Bake for 35–40 minutes, then leave to stand for 5 minutes.

4   Meanwhile, make the chocolate sauce. Place the chocolate and butter in a bowl over a saucepan of hot water and stir until melted. Add the milk and rum and stir for 1 minute.

5   Turn out the cake and sprinkle with chocolate shavings. Serve with the chocolate sauce poured over.

100 g ready-to-eat dried figs, chopped

4 tablespoons maple syrup

100 g unsalted butter, softened, plus extra for greasing

100 g light muscovado sugar

3 eggs, lightly beaten

75 g self-raising flour

1 teaspoon baking powder

1 tablespoon cocoa powder

100 g plain chocolate, melted

75 g fresh white breadcrumbs

Chocolate shavings, for sprinkling

FOR THE CHOCOLATE SAUCE

125 g plain chocolate

25 g butter

1 tablespoon full-fat milk

1 tablespoon rum

Serves 6

DATES STUFFED WITH RICOTTA

50 g ricotta cheese

1 tablespoon icing sugar

6 fresh dates

15 g pistachio nuts, chopped

Serves 2

This sweet treat makes a light dessert that is perfect for after a heavy meal. The cool, creamy ricotta cheese provides a delicious complement to the sweetness of the dates.

1 Mix the ricotta and icing sugar together in a small bowl.

2 Make a lengthways cut in each date and remove the stone.

3 Spoon a little of the ricotta mixture into the centre of each date. Sprinkle over a few chopped pistachio nuts and serve.

BRANDIED PRUNES WITH GREEK YOGURT

225 g pitted ready-to-eat dried prunes

50 g large seedless raisins

150 ml cold tea

3 tablespoons brandy

8 tablespoons Greek yogurt

2 tablespoons icing sugar

6 brandy snaps, to serve

Serves 6

Plump and succulent prunes make a light and tasty dessert. Prunes are a good source of fibre and provide useful amounts of calcium and iron.

1 Place the prunes and raisins in a large bowl and pour over the tea and brandy. Cover and leave to soak for at least 6 hours, or preferably overnight.

2 When ready to serve, beat together the Greek yogurt and icing sugar. Spoon the brandied prunes into serving bowls and top each with a spoonful of the yogurt mixture and a brandy snap.

LEMON & STRAWBERRY CHEESECAKE

This fresh, lemony cheesecake makes a perfect dinner party dessert or a snack with morning coffee.

1. To make the base, place the biscuits in a plastic bag, seal, then crush with a rolling pin to make fine crumbs. Melt the butter in a saucepan, then stir in the biscuit crumbs and demerara sugar. Press the mixture into the base and sides of a 20 cm loose-bottomed flan tin and chill until set.

2. To make the filling, place the lemon zest in a bowl. Add the cream cheese and condensed milk and beat until smooth. Very gradually beat in the lemon juice until the mixture is thick and creamy. In another bowl, whip the cream until it forms soft peaks, then fold into the cream cheese mixture.

3. Spoon the cheesecake mixture into the biscuit base and swirl the top with the back of a spoon. Arrange the strawberries cut-side down around the edge and chill for 1 hour.

4. For the strawberry sauce, put 225 g of the strawberries into a bowl and stir in the sugar and orange liqueur. Chill for 1 hour, then blend in a food processor or blender until smooth. Pass the purée through a fine nylon sieve to remove the seeds, then stir in the remaining strawberries and the orange zest.

5. To serve, remove the cheesecake from the tin and slice. Decorate with mint sprigs and serve with the strawberry sauce.

LEMON & RASPBERRY CHEESECAKE
Replace the strawberries with raspberries in both the filling and the sauce.

FOR THE CHEESECAKE BASE

225 g digestive biscuits

125 g butter

1 tablespoon demerara sugar

FOR THE FILLING

Zest of 1 lemon

225 g full-fat cream cheese

215 g canned sweetened condensed milk

Juice of 3 lemons

140 ml double cream

125 g fresh strawberries, cut in half

FOR THE STRAWBERRY SAUCE

450 g small ripe strawberries, cut into quarters

50 g caster sugar

2 tablespoons orange-flavoured liqueur

Zest of 1 orange

Fresh mint sprigs, to decorate

Serves 6–8

CARAMEL ORANGES WITH ALMOND & SESAME SEED BISCUITS

Oranges are a useful source of calcium and also provide plenty of other vitamins and minerals, especially vitamin C. These biscuits make a light, low-fat, tasty dessert.

1 Remove the zest from 3 of the oranges and reserve. To peel the oranges, slice them all across the top and bottom to reveal the flesh, then remove the skin and pith in strips by slicing downwards, following the shape of the orange.

2 Working over a bowl, remove the orange segments by slicing carefully between each segment and its membrane. Reserve the juice in the bowl. Put the orange segments to one side.

3 To make the orange caramel, put the sugar in a heavy-based saucepan with 3 tablespoons of water. Heat gently until the sugar dissolves, then bring to a rapid boil until it turns a rich, golden colour.

4 Remove from the heat and carefully add the honey, the reserved orange juice and half the reserved orange zest. The caramel will form a blob on the bottom of the pan, so return to a gentle heat and dissolve in the juice. When the mixture is smooth, set aside to cool.

5 When cool, pour the caramel over the orange segments. Chill in the fridge until ready to serve.

6 Meanwhile, make the almond sesame biscuits. Preheat the oven to 220°C, gas mark 7. Whisk the egg whites until stiff, then add the sugar and whisk for 1 minute until the mixture is glossy. Using a metal spoon, fold in the flour, butter, sesame seeds, almonds and the reserved orange zest.

7 Put teaspoons of the mixture onto a baking tray lined with baking parchment, about 6 cm apart. Bake for 5–6 minutes until golden, then remove from the oven. While the biscuits are still warm, press with a rolling pin to curve them – they will harden in seconds. If the biscuits harden before shaping, return to the oven for a few minutes to soften.

8 To serve, remove the orange segments from the fridge and spoon into serving bowls. Serve with the almond sesame biscuits.

FOR THE CARAMEL ORANGES

6 large oranges

200 g caster sugar

2 tablespoons runny honey

FOR THE ALMOND SESAME BISCUITS

2 egg whites

125 g caster sugar

50 g plain flour, sifted

50 g butter, melted

2 tablespoons sesame seeds

50 g blanched almonds, chopped

Serves 6 (makes around 24 biscuits)

MIXED BERRY BRULEE

This classic dish is made healthier by replacing the cream with lower-fat Greek yogurt.

125 g fresh blueberries

125 g fresh raspberries

125 g fresh strawberries, hulled and roughly chopped

Seeds and juice of 4 passion fruits

300 ml Greek yogurt

125 g soft brown sugar

Serves 4

1 Mix the blueberries, raspberries, strawberries and passion fruit seeds and juice together in a large bowl and divide between 4 ovenproof ramekins.

2 Spoon the yogurt over the fruit and chill for at least 2 hours.

3 Remove the ramekins from the fridge and sprinkle the sugar over the yogurt. Place under a hot grill until the sugar caramelises, then serve immediately.

LEMON & PASSION FRUIT ROULADE

Greek yogurt contains considerably less fat than double cream and about three times more calcium, helping to make this a healthier alternative to more traditional cream-filled desserts.

FOR THE MERINGUE

4 egg whites

225 g caster sugar

1 level tablespoon cornflour

2 teaspoons malt vinegar

1 teaspoon vanilla essence

FOR THE FILLING

4 tablespoons lemon curd

Seeds and juice of 4 passion fruits

25 g flaked almonds, toasted, to decorate

Icing sugar, for dusting

200 ml Greek yogurt

Serves 6

1 Preheat the oven to 150°C, gas mark 2. Line the base and sides of a 31.5 × 21.5 cm Swiss roll tin with non-stick baking parchment.

2 With an electric whisk, beat the egg whites until they are frothy and have doubled in bulk, then gradually whisk in the sugar until the mixture is very thick and shiny. Whisk in the cornflour, vinegar and vanilla essence.

3 Spoon the mixture into the prepared tin and level the surface. Bake for 50 minutes, or until the surface is just firm.

4 Meanwhile, to make the filling, mix together the lemon curd and passion fruit seeds and juice.

5 Remove the meringue from the oven and allow to cool for 10 minutes. Turn out and carefully peel off the paper. Lightly dust a sheet of baking parchment with toasted almonds and icing sugar and place the meringue on the parchment. Spread the yogurt over the meringue, then drizzle the lemon and passion fruit mixture over the yogurt.

6 Using the parchment to help you, roll up the meringue from one of the long ends. Refrigerate for at least 30 minutes, or until ready to serve.

APRICOT RISOTTO

This dessert is a variation on traditional rice pudding – the fruity apricot coulis adds a healthy, modern twist.

1 Place the canned apricots in a blender or food processor and purée until smooth. Set to one side. Place the milk and sugar in a saucepan and gently heat, stirring occasionally, until the milk reaches simmering point. Reduce the heat and allow the milk to simmer.

2 Melt the butter in a large saucepan, add the rice and cook, stirring, for 1–2 minutes. Add the chopped apricots and cook for 1–2 minutes.

3 Add a ladle of the warm milk and cook, stirring continuously, until the liquid is absorbed. Continue adding the milk in the same way until all the milk is used and the rice is tender – this will take about 20 minutes.

4 Stir the puréed apricots into the rice, then spoon into bowls and decorate with toasted almonds.

400 g can apricots in natural juice, drained

1 litre full-fat milk

2 tablespoons caster sugar

15 g butter

150 g arborio rice

100 g ready-to eat dried apricots, roughly chopped

2 tablespoons flaked almonds, toasted

Serves 4

FROZEN STRAWBERRY YOGURT

500 g strawberries, hulled and roughly chopped

3 tablespoons apple juice

2 tablespoons crème de cassis (optional)

4 tablespoons icing sugar

500 ml Greek yogurt

Fresh fruit, to decorate

Serves 4

This is a healthy treat for a hot day. Although you can buy frozen yogurt in most supermarkets, if you have the time it is really worth making your own – once you've eaten home-made, shop-bought will never taste quite the same. The frozen yogurt can be stored for up to 2 weeks in the freezer.

1 Place the strawberries in a saucepan. Add the apple juice and gently warm, stirring occasionally, until the strawberries become soft and pulpy.

2 Press the strawberries through a nylon sieve and collect their juice in a large bowl. Discard the seeds. Allow to cool completely, then beat in the crème de cassis (if using), icing sugar and yogurt.

3 Pour the mixture into an ice-cream machine and churn until it becomes thick and frozen. If you don't have an ice-cream machine, transfer the mixture to a shallow freezerproof container. Freeze for at least 1 hour, or until the mixture begins to set around the edges. Remove the container from the freezer and beat the mixture until smooth, then return to the freezer. Freeze for another 30 minutes then beat again. Repeat the freezing and beating process two more times.

4 Transfer the frozen yogurt from the freezer to the fridge 20 minutes before serving. Decorate with fresh fruit to serve.

LEMON MASCARPONE ICE CREAM

500 g mascarpone cheese

1 tablespoon lemon juice

Zest of 2 lemons

125 g icing sugar

3 egg yolks

2 tablespoons orange-flavoured liqueur

Fresh berries, to serve

Serves 6

This is an ideal dessert for a dinner party, especially when served with a selection of fresh summer berries. Remember that raw eggs are not suitable for the elderly, pregnant women, young children or people who have immune deficiency disease.

1 Beat the mascarpone cheese, lemon juice and zest, icing sugar, egg yolks and orange-flavoured liqueur together in a large bowl, until smooth.

2 Freeze the mixture in an ice cream maker, if you have one, or in a freezerproof container. If you use a freezerproof container, beat the mixture at hourly intervals until the ice cream is frozen – this helps to prevent ice crystals forming and ensures an even-textured result.

3 Once frozen, remove the ice cream from the freezer and serve with fresh berries.

Home Bakes

7

This chapter offers a selection of savoury snacks, biscuits and cakes that make delicious treats at any time of day. The bakes feature ingredients such as cheese, nuts, seeds and fruit, which boost their calcium content, making them great for healthy bones.

SUN-DRIED TOMATO & PARMESAN CORN BREAD SQUARES

Serve this tasty bread with a bowl of steaming hot soup for a healthy and filling lunchtime snack.

1 large egg, beaten

200 ml Greek yogurt

25 g butter, melted

150 g fine cornmeal

25 g flour

1 tablespoon baking powder

1 teaspoon fresh rosemary, chopped

½ teaspoon salt

50 g sun-dried tomatoes in oil, roughly chopped

125 g canned sweetcorn, drained

50 g Parmesan cheese, freshly grated

Makes 9 squares

1 Preheat the oven to 180°C, gas mark 4. Line the bottom of an 18 cm square tin, approximately 3 cm deep, with non-stick baking parchment.

2 Mix the egg, yogurt and melted butter together. Stir in the cornmeal, flour, baking powder, rosemary and salt. Add the sun-dried tomatoes, sweetcorn and Parmesan and mix until thoroughly combined.

3 Turn the mixture into the prepared tin and bake for 30–40 minutes, or until a skewer inserted into the centre of the loaf comes out clean.

4 Allow to cool in the tin for 10 minutes then turn out onto a cooling rack. When the bread is completely cold, cut into squares.

CHEESE & WATERCRESS SCONES

Light and easy to make, these scones make a delicious daytime snack. Watercress is an excellent source of vitamin C and vitamin E and provides substantial amounts of folic acid, niacin and vitamin B6.

300 g self-raising white flour, sieved

1 teaspoon baking powder

50 g butter, diced

125 g watercress, chopped with stalks removed

125 g Gruyère cheese, grated

Salt and pepper, to taste

100 ml semi-skimmed milk, plus extra to glaze

Flour, for dusting

Makes 8 scones

1 Preheat the oven to 220°C, gas mark 7. Place the flour and baking powder in a large bowl. Rub in the butter with your fingertips, until the mixture resembles fine breadcrumbs.

2 Stir in the watercress, 75 g of the cheese and the seasoning. Add the milk and stir to form a smooth, soft dough.

3 Turn the dough out on to a well-floured surface and roll out to 2 cm thick. Using a 7.5 cm round cutter, cut out the scones. Press the trimmings together, re-roll and cut out more scones, until all the dough has been used.

4 Place the scones on a greased baking sheet. Brush the tops with milk, sprinkle over the remaining cheese and bake for 10–15 minutes, or until golden brown. Transfer to a wire rack to cool.

PARMESAN & HERB TWISTS

These tasty little snacks are the perfect accompaniment for a glass of chilled white wine, and can also be served with dips or soups. They will keep for up to one week in an air-tight container.

1   Preheat the oven to 220°C, gas mark 7. Dust the work surface and rolling pin with a little flour. Roll out the pastry until it is very thin, then trim into a neat rectangle or square. Cut in half.

2   Sprinkle one half of the pastry with an even layer of Parmesan cheese, chopped rosemary and thyme. Dampen the edges, then carefully place the other piece of pastry on top and gently press down.

3   Using a kitchen knife, cut the Parmesan and herb pastry into strips. Twist each strip around a few times, then place on a baking sheet. Press the ends of the twists down so that they stick to the baking sheet – this stops them unwinding as they cook.

4   Bake the twists for about 10–12 minutes, or until golden brown, then remove the baking sheet from the oven. Leave them on the baking sheet for 5 minutes, then place on a wire rack to cool.

Plain flour, for dusting

500 g ready-made puff pastry

25 g Parmesan cheese, grated

2 tablespoons fresh rosemary, chopped

1 tablespoon fresh thyme leaves, chopped

Makes about 24 twists

PESTO & PARMESAN TWISTS
Replace the rosemary and thyme with 3 tablespoons of green pesto (see recipe page 48). Spread the pesto over one half of the pastry and sprinkle with Parmesan. Then follow steps 3 and 4 as above.

Soda Bread

350 g plain wholemeal flour

125 g pinhead oatmeal

2 teaspoons bicarbonate of soda

1 teaspoon salt

1 teaspoon sugar

300 ml buttermilk

3–4 tablespoons semi-skimmed milk

Makes 1 loaf

This classic Irish recipe is extremely healthy and couldn't be easier to make. It's delicious served warm with slices of mature cheddar cheese.

1 Preheat the oven to 200°C, gas mark 6. Place the flour, oatmeal, bicarbonate of soda, salt and sugar in a large bowl. Make a well in the centre and gradually beat in the buttermilk and enough milk to form a soft dough.

2 Knead the dough for 5 minutes, or until smooth. Shape into a round about 20 cm in diameter. Using a sharp knife, cut a deep cross on the top of the dough. Place on a non-stick baking tray.

3 Bake for 30–40 minutes or until the bread sounds hollow when tapped on the bottom. Serve warm or leave to cool on a wire rack.

Banana & Pumpkin Loaf

100 ml sunflower oil, plus extra for greasing

125 g self-raising flour

75 g self-raising wholemeal flour

½ teaspoon bicarbonate of soda

1 teaspoon ground cinnamon

100 g soft brown sugar

4 tablespoons buttermilk or plain yogurt

2 eggs, beaten

250 g pumpkin, coarsely grated

1 medium banana, mashed

125 g sultanas

Makes 1 loaf

This moist fruity loaf is delicious served plain, but for a special treat, try adding the mascarpone topping on page 123.

1 Preheat the oven to 180°C, gas mark 4. Lightly grease and line the base of a 900 g loaf tin with non-stick baking parchment.

2 Sift the flours, bicarbonate of soda and cinnamon into a large bowl. Stir in the sugar. Place the oil, buttermilk or yogurt and eggs in a separate bowl and whisk to combine. Pour the liquid into the flour and beat with an electric whisk for 1 minute.

3 Stir in the pumpkin, banana and sultanas and transfer the mixture to the prepared tin. Bake for 1 hour, or until a skewer inserted into the middle comes out clean. Allow to cool in the tin for 5–10 minutes, then carefully transfer to a wire rack to cool completely.

SESAME OAT CRISPS

Sesame seeds are a good source of calcium and vitamin E and give these biscuits a delicious nutty flavour.

1 Preheat the oven to 180°C, gas mark 4. Lightly grease 2 baking sheets.

2 Place the butter, syrup and sugar in a large saucepan. Heat the mixture gently, stirring occasionally, until the butter melts and the sugar dissolves.

3 Stir in the porridge oats, sesame seeds and flour and mix well.

4 Dissolve the bicarbonate of soda in 1 teaspoon of hot water and stir into the mixture.

5 Allow the mixture to cool slightly, then roll into walnut-sized balls. Place on the prepared baking sheets, allowing plenty of space for the mixture to spread as it bakes (you may need to cook the crisps in batches). Bake for 15 minutes, or until evenly browned.

6 Remove the crisps from the oven and leave on the baking sheets to cool slightly. Using a palette knife, transfer to a wire rack to cool completely.

125 g butter, plus extra for greasing

1 heaped tablespoon golden syrup

125 g demerara sugar

75 g porridge oats

50 g sesame seeds

125 g plain white flour

1 teaspoon bicarbonate of soda

Makes about 26 crisps

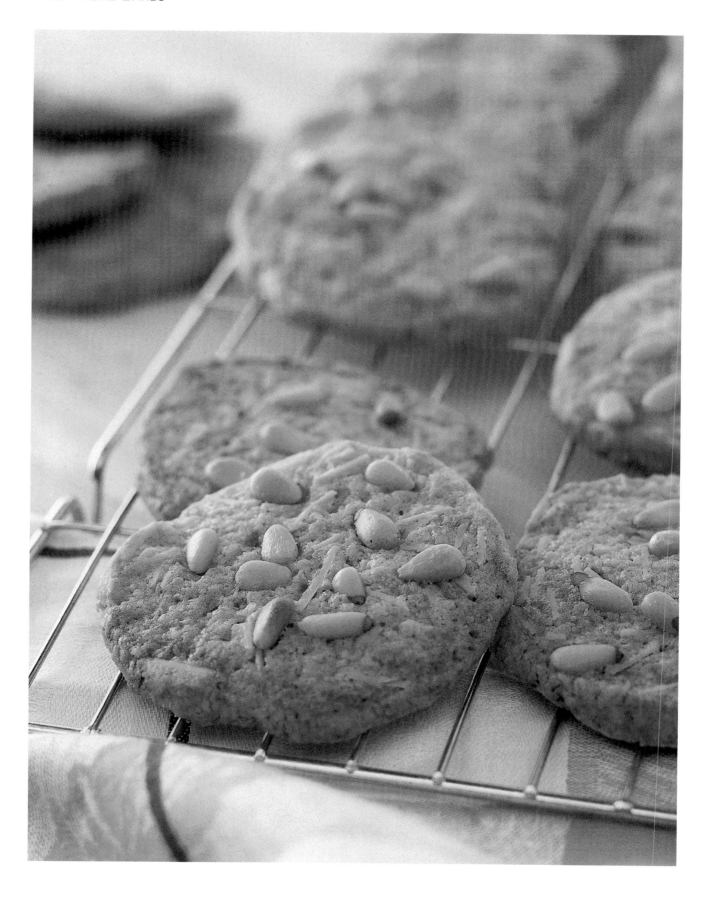

ALMOND & PINE NUT COOKIES

Nuts are a good source of B vitamins and minerals, making these cookies a healthy and tasty treat.

1 Preheat the oven to 190°C, gas mark 5. Lightly grease 2 baking sheets.

2 Sift the flour and bicarbonate of soda into a bowl. Add the butter and rub it in with your fingertips until the mixture resembles fine breadcrumbs. Add the sugar and almonds, then stir in the egg, orange zest and almond extract and mix to a dough, adding a little milk if necessary.

3 Turn out onto a lightly floured surface and shape into a cylinder about 23 cm long. Cut into thin slices and place on the baking sheets. Sprinkle over the pine nuts, pressing them down lightly with your fingertips.

4 Bake the cookies for 8–10 minutes until pale golden (you may need to cook them in batches). Allow to cool slightly before lifting them onto a wire rack, then leave to cool completely.

200 g plain flour, plus extra for dusting

½ teaspoon bicarbonate of soda

125 g butter, diced

125 g golden caster sugar

75 g flaked almonds, roughly chopped

1 egg, lightly beaten

Zest of 1 orange

Few drops almond extract

2 tablespoons milk

50 g pine nuts, finely chopped

Makes 27 cookies

APRICOT & PINE NUT COOKIES
Replace the almonds with 50 g finely chopped, ready-to-eat dried apricots. Follow the recipe as above, omitting the almond extract.

APRICOT & ORANGE MUFFINS

175 g plain white flour

2 teaspoons baking powder

Pinch salt

25 g golden caster sugar

2 tablespoons runny honey

1 egg

75 ml orange juice

75 ml full-fat milk

50 g butter, melted and cooled

50 g ready-to-eat dried apricots, chopped

Makes 6 muffins

These light-as-air muffins are studded with chewy apricots and orange zest. For a treat, they can also be served at breakfast.

1   Preheat the oven to 200°C, gas mark 6. Line 6 deep muffin tins with paper cases.

2   Sieve the flour, baking powder and salt into a large bowl. In another large bowl, mix together the sugar, honey, egg, orange juice, milk and cooled butter. Sieve the dry ingredients into the egg mixture and fold in gently with a metal spoon. Do not beat or whisk the mixture.

3   Lightly fold in the chopped apricots. then divide the mixture equally between the paper cases. Bake for 15 minutes, or until well-risen and golden brown. A skewer inserted into the centre of the muffins should come out clean. Leave in the tin for a few minutes, then transfer to a wire rack to cool. Serve warm or cold.

CITRUS YOGURT CAKE

200 ml natural yogurt

225 g golden caster sugar

125 g butter, melted, plus extra for greasing

3 eggs

Zest of ½ lemon, grated

Zest of ½ orange, grated

Zest of 1 lime, grated

350 g plain flour

FOR THE MASCARPONE CREAM

250 g mascarpone cheese

1 tablespoon orange thin-cut marmalade

Icing sugar, for dusting

Serves 8

This moist citrus cake is made with natural yogurt and served with a lovely mascarpone cream. Another way to serve this cake is to split it in half and sandwich the two halves together with the mascarpone cream, then dredge the top with icing sugar.

1   Preheat the oven to 180°C, gas mark 4. Lightly grease a 20 cm loose bottomed shallow cake tin and line the base with greaseproof paper.

2   In a large bowl, whisk together the yogurt, sugar, melted butter, eggs, lemon and orange and lime zest. Beat in the flour until well mixed.

3   Pour the cake mixture into the prepared tin and bake in the centre of the oven for 45–50 minutes, or until a skewer inserted into the centre of the cake comes out clean. Leave to cool for 10 minutes, then transfer to a cake rack to cool completely.

4   Meanwhile, beat the mascarpone with the marmalade. Cover and chill until ready to use.

5   Dust the top of the cake with icing sugar. Cut into wedges and serve with a spoonful of the mascarpone cream.

LEMON & POPPY SEED DRIZZLE LOAF CAKE

Poppy seeds are a useful source of calcium, particularly for people on dairy-free diets. This cake is good on its own or with a spoonful of crème fraîche or Greek yogurt.

1 Preheat the oven to 180°C, gas mark 4. Grease and line a 1.4 litre loaf tin.

2 Place the butter or margarine, sugar, eggs, flour, baking powder, salt, lemon zest and juice into a food processor and process until smooth. Fold in the poppy seeds.

3 Spoon the mixture into the prepared tin and level the surface. Bake for 50–55 minutes, or until well-risen and firm to the touch. Turn out and cool on a wire rack.

4 For the topping, mix the icing sugar with enough lemon juice to form a smooth consistency. Drizzle over the top of the cake and decorate with the shredded candied lemon peel.

FOR THE CAKE

225 g butter or margarine

175 g golden caster sugar

3 eggs

350 g self-raising wholemeal flour

1 teaspoon baking powder

Pinch salt

Zest and juice of 2 large lemons

50 g poppy seeds

FOR THE TOPPING

75 g icing sugar

2–3 teaspoons lemon juice

Candied lemon peel, shredded, to decorate

Makes 12 slices

RICH CHOCOLATE CAKE

200 g dark chocolate (about 70 per cent cocoa solid)

2 teaspoons instant coffee granules

200 g unsalted butter, softened

200 g caster sugar

4 eggs, separated

150 g ground almonds

75 g cornflour

Icing sugar, for dusting

Crème fraîche, to serve

Serves 10

This moist, rich chocolate cake not only tastes fantastic but, thanks to the ground almonds, is also a good source of calcium. Serve with Greek yogurt or reduced-fat crème fraîche.

1 Preheat the oven to 180°C, gas mark 4. Lightly grease a 20 cm loose bottomed shallow cake tin and line the base with greaseproof paper.

2 Place the chocolate and coffee in a bowl over a pan of simmering water and melt. In a large bowl, cream the butter and sugar until pale and fluffy. Beat in the eggs yolks, one at a time, then stir in the chocolate and coffee mixture, almonds and cornflour.

3 In a large clean bowl, whisk the egg whites until they form soft peaks. Fold a quarter of the whisked egg whites into the chocolate mixture to loosen it, then gradually fold in the remainder. Pour the mixture into the prepared tin and bake for 50–60 minutes, or until it springs back when touched. Cover the cake with greaseproof paper after 50 minutes. Allow to cool completely before carefully removing it from the tin.

4 Cut the cake into wedges, dust with a little icing sugar and serve with crème fraîche, if liked.

CARROT CAKE WITH MASCARPONE TOPPING

FOR THE CARROT CAKE

Butter, for greasing

Flour, for dusting

225 g unsalted butter or margarine, softened

225 g golden caster sugar

175 g self-raising white flour

1 teaspoon baking powder

½ teaspoon ground allspice

4 eggs

Zest of 1 large orange

This cake is guaranteed to be a hit with both children and adults. The mascarpone cheese makes a deliciously rich and creamy frosting.

1 Preheat the oven to 180°C, gas mark 4. Grease two 20 cm sandwich tins. Dust the sides of the tins with flour and shake out the excess.

2 Cream the butter or margarine and sugar together in a bowl until pale and fluffy. Sift the flour, baking powder and allspice into the bowl. Add the eggs, orange rind and juice and ground almonds and beat well, then stir in the walnuts and the carrots.

3 Divide the mixture equally between the two tins and level the surface. Bake for 35–40 minutes until the cakes have risen and are firm to the touch. Leave in the tins for 5 minutes, then transfer to a wire rack to cool.

4   For the topping, beat the mascarpone cheese and icing sugar together in a bowl until smooth. Use half of the mixture to sandwich the cake together, then spread the remaining mixture over the top of the cake. Arrange the walnut halves around the edge of the cake to decorate.

ORANGE MASCARPONE TOPPING

Beat together 500 g mascarpone cheese with 1 teaspoon orange zest, 2 tablespoons orange juice and 2 tablespoons icing sugar. Use to sandwich the cake together and spread the remainder over the top of the cake. Decorate with walnuts and orange zest.

1 tablespoon orange juice

50 g ground almonds

200 g carrots, finely grated

125 g walnuts, coarsely chopped

FOR THE MASCARPONE TOPPING

500 g mascarpone cheese

2 tablespoons icing sugar

50 g walnut halves, to decorate

Serves 8–10

The nutritional information for each recipe refers to a single serving, unless otherwise stated. Optional ingredients are not included. The figures are intended as a guide only. If salt is given in a measured amount in the recipe, it has been included in the analysis; if the recipe suggests adding a pinch of salt or seasoning to taste, salt has not been included.

p.12 Sweet Fruit Porridge
calories 235; KJ 996; protein 6g; fat 4g; saturated fat 1g; fibre 3g; sodium 50mg; calcium 75mg

p.12 Apple & Blueberry Muesli
calories 460–306; KJ 1944–1296; protein 15–10g; fat 13–9g; saturated fat 1g; fibre 7.5–5g; sodium 127–85mg; calcium 330–220mg

p.13 Spiced Fruit Compote
calories 340; KJ 1452; protein 7g; fat 9g; saturated fat 3g; fibre 5g; sodium 293mg; calcium 143mg

p.14 Dried Fruit Spread
calories 40; KJ 152; protein 1g; fat 0g; saturated fat 0g; fibre 1g; sodium 6mg; calcium 25mg

p.14 Bagels with Raspberries & Ricotta
calories 300; KJ 1220; protein 12g; fat 6g; saturated fat 3g; fibre 3g; sodium 40mg; calcium 100mg

p.14 Banana & Almond Smoothie
calories 320; KJ 1350; protein 13g; fat 15g; saturated fat 4g; fibre 3g; sodium 128mg; calcium 325mg

p.15 Apricot & Orange Smoothie
calories 170; KJ 727; protein 3g; fat 1g; saturated fat 0g; fibre 4g; sodium 29mg; calcium 65mg

p.15 Strawberry Smoothie
calories 100; KJ 410; protein 6g; fat 3g; saturated fat 0.5g; fibre 2g; sodium 60mg; calcium 70mg

p.17 Cheesy Scrambled Eggs
calories 300; KJ 1270; protein 22g; fat 23g; saturated fat 10g; fibre 0g; sodium 365mg; calcium 268mg

p.17 Smoked Haddock Omelette
calories 390; KJ 1629; protein 36g; fat 27g; saturated fat 12g; fibre 0g; sodium 1136mg; calcium 317mg

p.18 Soft Eggs with Soured Cream & Smoked Salmon
calories 310; KJ 1295; protein 19g; fat 18g; saturated fat 8g; fibre 1g; sodium 779mg; calcium 113mg

p.19 Smoked Haddock & Sweetcorn Fritters
calories 244; KJ 1036; protein 17g; fat 5g; saturated fat 1g; fibre 3g; sodium 733mg; calcium 128mg

p.19 Stuffed Portobello Mushrooms
calories 400; KJ 1199; protein 24g; fat 11g; saturated fat 3g; fibre 4.5g; sodium 1199mg; calcium 250mg

p.22 Broccoli & Stilton Soup
calories 275; KJ 1148; protein 16g; fat 16g; saturated fat 8g; fibre 4g; sodium 525mg; calcium 265mg

p.22 Moroccan Spiced Chickpea Soup
calories 210; KJ 876; protein 10g; fat 9g; saturated fat 1g; fibre 6g; sodium 440mg; calcium 90mg

p.23 Roasted Pepper Soup with Feta & Basil
calories 140; KJ 580; protein 5g; fat 8g; saturated fat 3g; fibre 3g; sodium 392mg; calcium 90mg

p.25 French Onion Soup
calories 370; KJ 1547; protein 13g; fat 18g; saturated fat 10g; fibre 3g; sodium 869mg; calcium 288mg

p.25 Garden Pea & Watercress Soup
calories 380; KJ 1605; protein 12g; fat 27g; saturated fat 7g; fibre 7g; sodium 545mg; calcium 118mg

p.26 Smoked Haddock & Sweetcorn Chowder
calories 390; KJ 1638; protein 35g; fat 9g; saturated fat 5g; fibre 3g; sodium 1865mg; calcium 205mg

p.26 Baked Ricotta with Roasted Vine Tomatoes
calories 350; KJ 14560; protein 24g; fat 26g; saturated fat 14g; fibre 1g; sodium 484mg; calcium 578mg

p.27 Mushroom & Goat's Cheese in Aubergine Parcels
calories 260; KJ 1062; protein 11g; fat 22g; saturated fat 8g; fibre 4g; sodium 301mg; calcium 144mg

p.28 Cherry Tomato & Goat's Cheese Tartlets
calories 440; KJ 1838; protein 13g; fat 32g; saturated fat 10g; fibre 0.5g; sodium 398mg; calcium 200mg

p.28 Tomato & Mozzarella Salad
calories 390; KJ 1622; protein 20g; fat 33g; saturated fat 12g; fibre 1.5g; sodium 471mg; calcium 453mg

p.29 Watercress, Pear & Roquefort Salad
calories 425; KJ 1763; protein 14g; fat 37g; saturated fat 13g; fibre 3g; sodium 857mg; calcium 367mg

p.29 Avocado & Smoked Salmon Rolls
calories 350; KJ 1476; protein 25g; fat 27g; saturated fat 10g; fibre 2g; sodium 1473mg; calcium 140mg

p.30 Roasted Red Pepper Dip
calories 135–90; KJ 570–380; protein 18–12g; fat 1–4.5g; saturated fat 0g; fibre 2–1g; sodium 188–125mg; calcium 150–100mg

p.30 Tzatziki
calories 125–83; KJ 512–341; protein 7–5g; fat 9–6g; saturated fat 5–3.5g; fibre 0.5g; sodium 74–50mg; calcium 166–111mg

p.30 Creamy Guacamole
calories 200; KJ 892; protein 3g; fat 21g; saturated fat 5g; fibre 4g; sodium 21mg; calcium 40mg

p.34 Humous
calories 275; KJ 1144; protein 9g; fat 21g; saturated fat 3g; fibre 5g; sodium 196mg; calcium 140mg

p.34 Red Pepper Humous
calories 280; KJ 1184; protein 10g; fat 19g; saturated fat 3g; fibre 6g; sodium 196mg; calcium 122mg

p.35 Falafel with Salad in Pitta
calories 485; KJ 2050; protein 20g; fat 12g; saturated fat 1g; fibre 6g; sodium 905mg; calcium 205mg

p.36 Quick Ciabatta Pizza
calories 300; KJ 1241; protein 11g; fat 15g; saturated fat 5g; fibre 2g; sodium 440mg; calcium 130mg

p.36 Croque Monsieur
calories 555; KJ 2341; protein 23g; fat 36g; saturated fat 19g; fibre 1g; sodium 1012mg; calcium 554mg

p.38 Peppered Smoked Mackerel Spread
calories 342; KJ 1419; protein 19g; fat 29g; saturated fat 9g; fibre 0g; sodium 751mg; calcium 110mg

p.38 Chcken Tikka Salad
calories 290; KJ 1205; protein 29g; fat 18g; saturated fat 4g; fibre 1g; sodium 177mg; calcium 70mg

p.39 Chicken Caesar Salad with Parmesan Crisps
calories 425; KJ 1775; protein 38g; fat 23g; saturated fat 6g; fibre 1g; sodium 593mg; calcium 280mg

p.40 Feta Omelette with Rocket & Red Pepper
calories 500; KJ 2095; protein 28g; fat 41g; saturated fat 19g; fibre 1.5g; sodium 1315mg; calcium 356mg

p.40 Twice Baked Goat's Cheese Soufflé
calories 210; KJ 875; protein 9g; fat 16g; saturated fat 10g; fibre 0g; sodium 343mg; calcium 225mg

p.42 Spinach & Roquefort Pancakes
calories 430; KJ 1796; protein 22g; fat 25g; saturated fat 13g; fibre 4g; sodium 1294mg; calcium 654mg

p.42 Cajun Cheese Potato Skins with Tomato & Red Onion Salad
calories 300; KJ 1271; protein 12g; fat 14g; saturated fat 7g; fibre 2g; sodium 223mg; calcium 235mg

p.44 Bacon & Ricotta Tart
calories 400; KJ 1676; protein 18g; fat 20g; saturated fat 10g; fibre 2g; sodium 1255mg; calcium 229mg

p.45 Sweet Potato with Cottage Cheese & Crispy Bacon
calories 390; KJ 1652; protein 27g; fat 8g; saturated fat 4g; fibre 6g; sodium 1415mg; calcium 138mg

p.45 Spinach & Potato Cake
calories 420; KJ 1750; protein 18g; fat 24g; saturated fat 13g; fibre 4g; sodium 330mg; calcium 366g

p.48 Brie-stuffed Chicken with Creamy Pesto
calories 460; KJ 1931; protein 47g; fat 28g; saturated fat 13g; fibre 0g; sodium 937mg; calcium 300mg

p.49 Chicken & Wild Mushroom Stroganoff
calories 380; KJ 1568; protein 35g; fat 22g; saturated fat 10g; fibre 2g; sodium 388mg; calcium 27mg

p.49 Garlic Chicken in Yogurt
calories 440; KJ 1813; protein 29g; fat 34g; saturated fat 8g; fibre 2g; sodium 173mg; calcium 200mg

p.50 Coronation Chicken Salad
calories 760–506; KJ 3158–2105; protein 40–27g; fat 52–35g; saturated fat 15–10g; fibre 3–2g; sodium 565–376mg; calcium 115–77mg

p 51 Chicken & Sesame Bites
calories 300; KJ 1248; protein 23g; fat 17g; saturated fat 3g; fibre 2g; sodium 228mg; calcium 166mg

p.51 Quick Turkey Cassoulet
calories 560; KJ 2374; protein 58g; fat 15g; saturated fat 5g; fibre 12g; sodium 2318mg; calcium 336mg

p.52 Pork Stuffed with Apricots & Pine Nuts
calories 555–370; KJ 2320–1547; protein 53–35g; fat 29–19g; saturated fat 8–5g; fibre 2–1g; sodium 525–350mg; calcium 85–57mg

p.54 Pork with Pak Choi & Black Bean Sauce
calories 540; KJ 2273; protein 37g; fat 22g; saturated fat 5g; fibre 5g; sodium 1785mg; calcium 190mg

p.54 Pork Escalopes with Celeriac Cream Mash
calories 5116; KJ 2153; protein 31g; fat 29g; saturated fat 6g; fibre 6g; sodium 348mg; calcium 88mg

p.56 Polenta with Bacon & Mushrooms
calories 480; KJ 2000; protein 32g; fat 24g; saturated fat 11g; fibre 2g; sodium 1622mg; calcium 431mg

p.57 Broccoli & Smoked Ham Tagliatelle
calories 850; KJ 3557; protein 33g; fat 48g; saturated fat 29g; fibre 9g; sodium 1033mg; calcium 369mg

p.58 Skewered Lamb with Tomato, Chilli & Yogurt Marinade
calories 600; KJ 2500; protein 43g; fat 24g; saturated fat 8g; fibre 0g; sodium 275mg; calcium 75mg

p.59 Garlic & Cumin Roast Lamb with Chickpea & Apricot Salsa
calories 460; KJ 1919; protein 42g; fat 22g; saturated fat 8g; fibre 5g; sodium 334mg; calcium 70mg

p.60 Moroccan Lamb with Chickpea & Apricots
calories 440; KJ 1841; protein 32g; fat 15g; saturated fat 5g; fibre 6g; sodium 492mg; calcium 90mg

p.61 Moussaka
calories 540; KJ 2241; protein 43g; fat 31g; saturated fat 14g; fibre 4g; sodium 460mg; calcium 424mg

p.62 Shepherd's Pie
calories 510; KJ 2142; protein 35g; fat 23g; saturated fat 12g; fibre 5g; sodium 344mg; calcium 210mg

p.62 Blue Cheese & Walnut Steaks
calories 480; KJ 2000; protein 45g; fat 33g; saturated fat 14g; fibre 0g; sodium 488mg; calcium 125mg

p.63 Meatballs with Mozzarella & Tomato Sauce
calories 470; KJ 1964; protein 38g; fat 24g; saturated fat 10g; fibre 2g; sodium 505mg; calcium 271mg

p.65 Minced Beef with Polenta Topping
calories 630; KJ 2612; protein 39g; fat 34g; saturated fat 12g; fibre 3g; sodium 666mg; calcium 311mg

p.66 Salmon Fish Cakes
calories 540; KJ 2260; protein 29g; fat 27g; saturated fat 4g; fibre 12g; sodium 850mg; calcium 367mg

p.66 Salmon & Leek Lasagne
calories 590; KJ 2454; protein 37g; fat 34g; saturated fat 18g; fibre 2g; sodium 744mg; calcium 785mg

p.67 Smoked Salmon & Dill Quiche
calories 500; KJ 2090; protein 13g; fat 41g; saturated fat 21g; fibre 1g; sodium 718mg; calcium 140mg

p.68 Quick Salmon Kedgeree
calories 420; KJ 1741; protein 23g; fat 16g; saturated fat 6g; fibre 0g; sodium 303mg; calcium 206mg

p.68 Salmon with a Crumb Crust
calories 380; KJ 1590; protein 30g; fat 25g; carbohydrate 10g; fibre 0g; sodium 382mg; calcium 200mg

p.69 Cod & Broccoli Cheese Pie
calories 894; KJ 3712; protein 39g; fat 65g; saturated fat 41g; fibre 4g; sodium 617mg; calcium 394mg

p.70 Cod Baked in Yogurt
calories 160; KJ 680; protein 34g; fat 1.5g; saturated fat 0g; fibre 0g; sodium 258mg; calcium 87mg

p.70 Poached Haddock with Spinach & Poached Egg
calories 270; KJ 1147; protein 42g; fat 10g; saturated fat 3g; fibre 3g; sodium 1423mg; calcium 350mg

p.71 Fish Pie with Rosti Topping
calories 615; KJ 2552; protein 22g; fat 46g; saturated fat 28g; fibre 3g; sodium 891mg; calcium 123mg

p.71 Deep-fried Whitebait
calories 550; KJ 2299; protein 16g; fat 52g; saturated fat 6g; fibre 0g; sodium 278mg; calcium 711mg

p.72 Monkfish Kebabs with Roasted Vegetables & Pesto
calories 480; KJ 2000; protein 31g; fat 35g; saturated fat 8g; fibre 4g; sodium 523mg; calcium 240mg

p.73 Griddled Swordfish with Salsa Verde
calories 330; KJ 1358; protein 36g; fat 23g; saturated fat 4g; fibre 0g; sodium 365mg; calcium 45mg

p.74 Prawn & Spinach Roulade
calories 400; KJ 1636; protein 15g; fat 33g; saturated fat 19g; fibre 1g; sodium 895mg; calcium 218mg

p.74 Penne with Prawns & Asparagus
calories 680; KJ 2864; protein 42g; fat 33g; saturated fat 8g; fibre 3g; sodium 1844mg; calcium 456mg

p.76 Warm Lentil & Feta Salad
calories 404; KJ 1691; protein 22g; fat 22g; saturated fat 9g; fibre 6g; sodium 734mg; calcium 225mg

p.77 Spiced Spinach Lentil & Feta Filo Pie
calories 481; KJ 2000; protein 22g; fat 11g; saturated fat 5g; fibre 6g; sodium 682mg; calcium 306mg

p.78 Cheese & Leek Sausages
calories 372; KJ 1552; protein 14g; fat 24g; saturated fat 8g; fibre 1g; sodium 405mg; calcium 255mg

p.78 Vegetable Patties
calories 507; KJ 2117; protein 23g; fat 2g; saturated fat 13g; fibre 4g; sodium 575mg; calcium 500mg

p.79 Spiced Tofu Burgers
calories 160; KJ 669; protein 8g; fat 9g; saturated fat 1g; fibre 2g; sodium 85mg; calcium 322mg

p.80 Roasted Thai-style Tofu with Stir-fried Vegetables
calories 290; KJ 1208; protein 15g; fat 17g; saturated fat 2g; fibre 5g; sodium 986mg; calcium 681mg

p.82 Marinated Tofu with Satay Sauce
calories 452; KJ 1877; protein 19g; fat 36g; saturated fat 7g; fibre 3g; sodium 772mg; calcium 348mg

p.83 Hot Spiced Chickpeas
calories 175; KJ 741; protein 9g; fat 5g; saturated fat 0.6g; fibre 6g; sodium 264mg; calcium 64mg

p.83 Chickpea & Potato Stew
calories 393; KJ 1654; protein 17g; fat 12g; saturated fat 1g; fibre 10g; sodium 693mg; calcium 149mg

p.84 Mixed Beans with a Cornmeal Topping
calories 544; KJ 2290; protein 30g; fat 18g; saturated fat 8g; fibre 13g; sodium 1955mg; calcium 438mg

p.85 Butternut Squash &
Gruyère Risotto
calories 537; KJ 2230; protein 17g;
fat 30g; saturated fat 13g;
fibre 3g; sodium 399mg;
calcium 373mg

p.87 Roasted Vegetable Lasagne
calories 473; KJ 1986; protein 25g;
fat 23g; saturated fat 11g;
fibre 5g; sodium 423mg;
calcium 505mg

p.87 Pappardelle with Spicy
Tomato Sauce & Ricotta
calories 392; KJ 1659; protein 15g;
fat 10g; saturated fat 4g; fibre 4g;
sodium 149mg; calcium 177mg

p.88 Broccoli & Gruyère Souffle
calories 245; KJ 1016; protein 13g;
fat 18g; saturated fat 10g;
fibre 1g; sodium 259mg;
calcium 286mg

p.89 Mediterranean Stuffed
Peppers with Coucous
calories 434; KJ 1802; protein 14g;
fat 26g; saturated fat 7g;
fibre 3.2g; sodium 864mg;
calcium 160mg

p.92 French Beans with Feta &
Sun-dried Tomatoes
calories 125; KJ 511; protein 4g;
fat 10g; saturated fat 3g; fibre 1g;
sodium 400mg; calcium 95mg

p.92 Roasted Baby Carrots with
Feta & Sun-dried Tomatoes
calories 160; KJ 670; protein 6g;
fat 10g; saturated fat 15g;
fibre 3g; sodium 202mg;
calcium 188mg

p.93 Asian-style Broccoli
calories 75; KJ 310; protein 5g; fat
5g; saturated fat 1g; fibre 3g;
sodium 224mg; calcium 72mg

p.94 Honeyed Parsnips with
Sesame Seeds
calories 250; KJ 1069; protein 4g;
fat 14g; saturated fat 7g;
fibre 8g; sodium 113mg;
calcium 125mg

p.95 Fantail Roast Potatoes with
Sesame Seeds
calories 304; KJ 1218; protein 7g;
fat 9g; saturated fat 1g; fibre 4g;
sodium 22mg; calcium 50mg

p.96 Sweet Potato & Anchovy
Gratin
calories 650; KJ 2707; protein 14g;
fat 50g; saturated fat 29g;
fibre 4g; sodium 610mg;
calcium 321mg

p.96 Aubergine & Tomato Gratin
calories 334; KJ 1384; protein 9g;
fat 31g; saturated fat16g; fibre 2g;
sodium 273mg; calcium 186mg

p.98 Cauliflower & Broccoli
Cheese
calories 520; KJ 2167; protein 13g;
fat 48g; saturated fat 29g;
fibre 3g; sodium 457mg;
calcium 296mg

p.98 Apple, Walnut &
Watercress Salad
calories 223; KJ 936; protein 3g;
fat 20g; saturated fat 2g; fibre 2g;
sodium 15mg; calcium 63mg

p.99 Potato Salad with Blue
Cheese Dressing
calories 250; KJ 1039; protein 11g;
fat 13g; saturated fat 8g;
fibre 2g; sodium 311mg;
calcium 136mg

p.102 Fudgy Nut Pie
calories 615; KJ 2580; protein 8g;
fat 32g; saturated fat 12g;
fibre 2g; sodium 470mg;
calcium 75mg

p.102 Spiced Apple & Raisin
Pancakes
calories 338; KJ 1434; protein 8g;
fat 5g; saturated fat 1.5g;
fibre 4g; sodium 172mg;
calcium 155mg

p.103 Rich Chocolate & Fig
Puddings with Chocolate Sauce
calories 6240; KJ 2612; protein
10g; fat 33g; saturated fat 19g;
fibre 2g; sodium 477mg; calcium
156mg

p.104 Dates Stuffed with Ricotta
calories 180; KJ 766; protein 4g;
fat 5g; saturated fat 2g; fibre 1.5g;
sodium 53mg; calcium 82mg

p.104 Brandied Prunes with
Crème Fraîche
calories 149; KJ 629; protein 3g;
fat 3g; saturated fat 2g; fibre 2g;
sodium 33mg; calcium 67mg

p.105 Lemon & Strawberry
Cheesecake
calories 800–600; KJ 3342–2507;
protein 8–6g; fat 57–43g;
saturated fat 34–26g;
fibre 2–1.5g; sodium 560–419mg;
calcium 206–154mg

p.107 Caramel Oranges with
Almond & Sesame Seed Biscuits
calories 455; KJ 1921; protein 6g;
fat 14g; saturated fat 5g; fibre 3g;
sodium 92mg; calcium 123mg

p.108 Mixed Berry Brulée
calories 240; KJ 1011; protein 6g;
fat 7g; saturated fat 4g;
fibre 1.5g; sodium 62mg;
calcium 130mg

p.108 Lemon & Passion Fruit
Roulade
calories 350; KJ 1465; protein 6g;
fat 15g; saturated fat 8g;
fibre 1g; sodium 84mg;
calcium 80mg

p.109 Apricot Risotto
calories 480; KJ 1996; protein 14g;
fat 17g; saturated fat 8g;
fibre 3g; sodium 175mg;
calcium 353mg

p.110 Frozen Strawberry Yogurt
calories 241; KJ 1008; protein 9g;
fat 11.5g; saturated fat 6g;
fibre 1g; sodium 100mg;
calcium 210mg

p.110 Lemon Mascarpone
Ice Cream
calories 490; KJ 2037; protein 4g;
fat 42g; saturated fat 25g;
fibre 0g; sodium 258mg;
calcium 94mg

p.114 Sun-dried Tomato &
Parmesan Corn Bread Squares
calories 200; KJ 830; protein 7g;
fat 10g; saturated fat 4g; fibre
0.5g; sodium 504mg;
calcium 130mg

p.114 Cheese & Watercress
Scones
calories 240; KJ 1025; protein 8g;
fat 11g; saturated fat 7g;
fibre 1g; sodium 375mg;
calcium 329mg

p.115 Parmesan & Herb Twists
calories 80; KJ 330; protein 1g;
fat 5g; saturated fat 0.5g;
fibre 0g; sodium 73mg;
calcium 24mg

p.116 Soda Bread
(per slice) calories 174; KJ 741;
protein 7g; fat 2g; saturated fat
0g; fibre 4g; sodium 493mg;
calcium 64mg

p.116 Banana & Pumpkin Loaf
(per slice) calories 240; KJ 1004;
protein 4g; fat 9g; saturated fat
1g; fibre 2g; sodium 137mg;
calcium 77mg

p.117 Sesame Oat Crisps
calories 100; KJ 415; protein 1g;
fat 6g; saturated fat 2g;
fibre 0.5g; sodium 95mg;
calcium 22mg

p.119 Almond & Pine Nut
Cookies
calories 111; KJ 462; protein 2g;
fat 7g; saturated fat 3g;
fibre 0.5g; sodium 64mg;
calcium 22mg

p.120 Apricot & Orange Muffins
calories 245; KJ 1031; protein 5g;
fat 9g; saturated fat 5g; fibre 1g;
sodium 365mg; calcium 90mg

p.120 Citrus Yogurt Cake
calories 565; KJ 2365; protein 9g;
fat 31g; saturated fat 18g;
fibre 1.5g; sodium 266mg;
calcium 156mg

p.121 Lemon & Poppy Seed
Drizzle Loaf Cake
calories 335; KJ 1399; protein 6g;
fat 19g; saturated fat 11g; fibre 3g;
sodium 254mg; calcium 94mg

p.122 Rich Chocolate Cake
calories 520; KJ 2155; protein 8g;
fat 36g; saturated fat 16g;
fibre 1.5g; sodium 193mg;
calcium 80mg

p.122 Carrot Cake with
Mascarpone Topping
calories 747; KJ 3103; protein 10g;
fat 60g; saturated fat 29g;
fibre 2g; sodium 427mg;
calcium 131mg

Index

Entries in italics denote
variations on the main recipes

Almond & Pine Nut
        Cookies 119
Apple
        Apple, Walnut & Watercress
                Salad 98
        & Blueberry Muesli 12
        Spiced Apple & Raisin
                Pancakes 102
Apricot
        & Orange Muffins 120
        & Orange Smoothie 15
        Risotto 109
Asian-style Broccoli 93
Aubergine & Tomato Gratin 96
Avocado & Smoked Salmon
        Rolls 29

Bacon & Ricotta Tart 44
Bagels with Raspberries &
        Ricotta 14
Baked Ricotta with Roasted Vine
        Tomatoes 26
Banana
        & Almond Smoothie 14
        & Pumpkin Loaf 116
Beef
        Blue Cheese & Walnut
                Steaks 62
        Meatballs with Mozzarella &
                Tomato Sauce 63
        Minced Beef with Polenta
                Topping 65
        Minced Beef with Olive & Stilton
                Polenta Topping 65
Biscuits
        Almond & Pine Nut
                Cookies 119
        Caramel Oranges with
                Almond & Sesame Seed
                Biscuits 107
        Sesame Oat Crisps 117
Blue Cheese
        Potato Salad with Blue Cheese
                Dressing 99
        Soufflés 41
        & Walnut Steaks 62
Brandied Prunes with Greek
        Yogurt 104
Breads
        Banana & Pumpkin Loaf 116
        Soda Bread 116
        Sun-dried Tomato & Parmesan
                Corn Bread Squares 114
Brie-stuffed Chicken with
        Creamy Pesto 48
Broccoli
        Asian-style Broccoli 93

Cauliflower & Broccoli
        Cheese 98
        Cod & Broccoli Cheese Pie 69
        & Gruyère Soufflé 88
        Salmon & Broccoli Cheese Pie 69
        & Smoked Ham Tagliatelle 57
        & Stilton Soup 22
Butternut Squash & Gruyère
        Risotto 85

Caesar Salad on Toasted Ciabatta 39
Cajun Cheese Potato Skins with
        Tomato & Red Onion
                Salad 42
Cakes
        Carrot Cake
                with Mascarpone
                Topping 122
                with Orange Mascarpone
                Topping 123
        Citrus Yogurt Cake 120
        Lemon & Poppy Seed Drizzle
                Loaf Cake 121
        Rich Chocolate Cake 122
Caramel Oranges with Almond
        & Sesame Seed Biscuits 107
Carrot Cake
        with Mascarpone
        Topping 122
        with Orange Mascarpone
        Topping 123
Cauliflower & Broccoli Cheese 98
Cheese & Leek Sausages 78
Cheese & Watercress Scones 114
Cheesy Scrambled Eggs 17
Cherry Tomato & Goat's Cheese
        Tartlets 28
Chicken
        Brie-stuffed Chicken with
                Creamy Pesto 48
        Caesar Salad with Parmesan
                Crisps 39
        Coronation Chicken Salad 50
        Garlic Chicken in Yogurt 49
        & Sesame Bites 51
        Tikka Salad 38
        & Wild Mushroom
                Stroganoff 49
Chickpea
        Hot Spiced Chickpeas 83
        Moroccan Spiced Chickpea
                Soup 22
        & Potato Stew 83
        & Sweet Potato Stew 83
Chocolate
        Fudgy Nut Pie 102
        Rich Chocolate Cake 122
        Rich Chocolate & Fig
                Puddings with Chocolate
                Sauce 103

Citrus Yogurt Cake 120
Cod
        & Broccoli Cheese Pie 69
        with Carrot Topping 69
        with Parsnip Topping 69
        Baked in Yogurt 70
Coronation Chicken Salad 50
Creamy Guacamole 30
Croque Monsieur 36

Dates Stuffed with Ricotta 104
Deep-fried Whitebait 71
Dips
        Creamy Guacamole 30
        Humous 34
        Red Pepper Humous 34
        Roasted Red Pepper Dip 30
        Tzatziki 30
Dried Fruit Spread 14

Egg(s)
        Cheesy Scrambled Eggs 17
        Feta Omelette with Rocket &
                Red Pepper 40
        Smoked Haddock Omelette 17
        Soft Eggs with Soured Cream
                & Smoked Salmon 18

Falafel with Salad in Pitta 35
Fantail Roast Potatoes with
        Sesame Seeds 95
Feta Omelette with Rocket & Red
        Pepper 40
Fish (*see also* individual fish)
        Deep-fried Whitebait 71
        Griddled Swordfish with Salsa
                Verde 73
        Monkfish Kebabs with
                Roasted Vegetables and
                Pesto 72
        Penne with Prawns &
                Asparagus 74
        Pie with Rosti Topping 71
        Prawn & Spinach Roulade 74
        Tuna Kedgeree 68
French Beans with Feta &
        Sun-dried Tomatoes 92
French Onion Soup 25
Fresh Pesto 48
Frozen Strawberry Yogurt 110
Fruit (*see also* individual fruit)
        Brandied Prunes with Greek
                Yogurt 104
        Caramel Oranges with
                Almond & Sesame Seed
                Biscuits 107
        Dates Stuffed with Ricotta 104
        Dried Fruit Spread 14
        Mixed Berry Brulée 108
        Spiced Fruit Compote 13

Fudgy Nut Pie 102
Garden Pea & Watercress Soup
        with Sesame Croutons 25
Garlic & Cumin Roasted Lamb
        with Apricot & Chickpea
        Salsa 59
Garlic Chicken in Yogurt 49
Griddled Swordfish with Salsa
        Verde 73
Grilled Vegetables with Satay
        Sauce 82

Haddock
        Poached Haddock with
                Spinach & Poached Egg 70
        Smoked Haddock &
                Sweetcorn Chowder 26
        Smoked Haddock &
                Sweetcorn Fritters 19
        Smoked Haddock Omelette 17
Home-made Caesar Salad
        Dressing 39
Home-made Cajun Seasoning 43
Honeyed Parsnips with Sesame
        Seeds 94
Hot Spiced Chickpeas 83
Humous 34

Ices
        Frozen Strawberry
                Yogurt 110
        Lemon Mascarpone Ice
                Cream 110

Lamb
        Garlic & Cumin Roasted Lamb
                with Apricot & Chickpea
                Salsa 59
        Moroccan Lamb with Butter
                Beans & Prunes 60
        Moroccan Lamb with
                Chickpeas & Apricots 60
        Moussaka 61
        Shepherd's Pie 62
        Skewered Lamb with Tomato,
                Chilli & Yogurt Marinade 58
Lemon
        & Passion Fruit Roulade 108
        & Poppy Seed Drizzle Loaf
                Cake 121
        & Raspberry Cheesecake 105
        & Strawberry Cheesecake 105
        Mascarpone Ice Cream 110

Marinated Tofu with Satay
        Sauce 82
Meatballs with Mozzarella &
        Tomato Sauce 63
Mediterranean Stuffed Peppers
        with Couscous 89

Mixed Beans with a Cornmeal Topping 84
Mixed Berry Brulée 108
Monkfish Kebabs with Roasted Vegetables & Pesto 72
Moroccan Lamb with Chickpeas & Apricots 60
Moroccan Lamb with Butter Beans & Prunes 60
Moroccan Spiced Chickpea Soup 22
Moussaka 61
Mushroom Polenta 56
Mushrooms & Goat's Cheese in Aubergine Parcels 27

Pappardelle with Spicy Tomato Sauce & Ricotta 87
Parmesan & Herb Twists 115
Parsnips with a Sweet Lime Glaze 94
Pasta
  Broccoli & Smoked Ham Tagliatelle 57
  Pappardelle with Spicy Tomato Sauce & Ricotta 87
  Penne with Prawns & Asparagus 74
  Pork with Pak Choi & Black Bean Sauce 54
  Vegetable Tagliatelle 56
Pastry
  Cherry Tomato & Goat's Cheese Tartlets 28
  Fudgy Nut Pie 102
  Parmesan & Herb Twists 115
  Pesto & Parmesan Twists 115
  Smoked Salmon & Dill Quiche 67
  Spiced Spinach, Lentil & Feta Filo Pie 77
Penne with Prawns & Asparagus 74
Peppered Smoked Mackerel Spread 38
Pesto & Parmesan Twists 115
Poached Haddock with Spinach & Poached Egg 70
Polenta with Bacon & Mushrooms 56
Pork
  Escalopes with Celeriac Cream Mash 54
  Stuffed with Apricots & Pine Nuts 52
  Stuffed with Apple & Walnuts 52
  with Pak Choi & Black Bean Sauce 54
Potato(es)
  Cajun Cheese Potato Skins with Tomato & Red Onion Salad 42
  Fantail Roast Potatoes with Sesame Seeds 95
  Fish Pie with Rosti Topping 71
  Red Pesto Fantail Roast Potatoes 95

Salad with Blue Cheese Dressing 99
Spinach & Potato Cake 45
Sweet Potato & Anchovy Gratin 96
Sweet Potato with Cottage Cheese & Crispy Bacon 45
Prawn & Spinach Roulade 74

Quick Ciabatta Pizza 36
Quick Salmon Kedgeree 68
Quick Turkey Cassoulet 51

Red Pepper Humous 34
Red Pesto Fantail Roast Potatoes 95
Rice
  Apricot Risotto 109
  Butternut Squash & Gruyère Risotto 85
  Quick Salmon Kedgeree 68
  Tuna Kedgeree 68
  Rich Chocolate & Fig Puddings with Chocolate Sauce 103
Rich Chocolate Cake 122
Roasted Baby Carrots with Parmesan & Coriander Topping 92
Roasted Pepper Soup with Feta & Basil 23
Roasted Red Pepper Dip 30
Roasted Thai-style Tofu with Stir-fried Vegetables 80
Roasted Vegetable Lasagne 87

Salads
  Apple, Walnut & Watercress Salad 98
  Caesar Salad on Toasted Ciabatta 39
  Cajun Cheese Potato Skins with Tomato & Red Onion Salad 42
  Coronation Chicken Salad 50
  Potato Salad with Blue Cheese Dressing 99
  Tomato & Mozzarella Salad 28
  Warm Lentil & Feta Salad 76
  Watercress, Pear & Roquefort Salad 29
Salmon
  Avocado & Smoked Salmon Rolls 29
  & Broccoli Cheese Pie 69
  Fish Cakes 66
  & Leek Lasagne 66
  Quick Salmon Kedgeree 68
  Smoked Salmon & Dill Quiche 67
  with a Crumb Crust 68
Sesame Oat Crisps 117
Shepherd's Pie 62
Skewered Lamb with Tomato, Chilli & Yogurt Marinade 58
Smoked Salmon & Dill Quiche 67
Smoothies
  Banana & Almond 14
  Apricot & Orange 15
  Strawberry 15
Soda Bread 116

Soft Eggs with Soured Cream & Smoked Salmon 18
Soufflés
  Blue Cheese 41
  Broccoli & Gruyère 88
  Spinach & Gruyère 88
  Twice-baked Goat's Cheese 40
Soups
  French Onion Soup 25
  Garden Pea & Watercress Soup with Sesame Croutons 25
  Moroccan Spiced Chickpea Soup 22
  Roasted Pepper Soup with Feta & Basil 23
Spiced Apple & Raisin Pancakes 102
Spiced Fruit Compote 13
Spiced Spinach, Lentil & Feta Filo Pie 77
Spiced Tofu Burgers 79
Spicy Roasted Baby Carrots with Feta 92
Spinach
  & Gruyère Soufflé 88
  Poached Haddock with Spinach & Poached Egg 70
  & Potato Cake 45
  Prawn & Spinach Roulade 74
  & Roquefort Pancakes 42
  Spiced Spinach, Lentil & Feta Filo Pie 77
Strawberry Smoothie 15
Stuffed Portobello Mushrooms 19
Sun-dried Tomato & Parmesan Corn Bread Squares 114
Sweet Fruit Porridge 12
Sweet Potato & Anchovy Gratin 96
Sweet Potato with Cottage Cheese & Crispy Bacon 45

Tofu
  Marinated Tofu with Satay Sauce 82
  Roasted Thai-style Tofu with Stir-fried Vegetables 80
  Spiced Tofu Burgers 79

Tomato(es)
  Aubergine & Tomato Gratin 96
  Baked Ricotta with Roasted Vine Tomatoes 26
  Cherry Tomato & Goat's Cheese Tartlets 28
  & Mozzarella Salad 28
Tuna Kedgeree 68
Twice-baked Goat's Cheese Soufflés 40
Tzatziki 30

Vegetable(s) (*see also* individual vegetables)
  Cauliflower & Broccoli Cheese 98
  French Beans with Feta & Sun-dried Tomatoes 92
  Grilled Vegetables with Satay Sauce 82
  Honeyed Parsnips with Sesame Seeds 94
  Mediterranean Stuffed Peppers with Couscous 89
  Mushroom Polenta 56
  Mushrooms & Goat's Cheese in Aubergine Parcels 27
  Parsnips with a Sweet Lime Glaze 94
  Patties 78
  Roasted Baby Carrots with Parmesan & Coriander Topping 92
  Roasted Vegetable Lasagne 87
  Spicy Roasted Baby Carrots with Feta 92
  Stuffed Portobello Mushrooms 19
  Tagliatelle 56

Warm Lentil & Feta Salad 76
Watercress, Pear & Roquefort Salad 29
Welsh Rarebit 36

ACKNOWLEDGEMENTS

Editorial assistance: Tom Broder
Nutritional analysis: Fiona Hunter
Production: Nigel Reed
IT: Paul Stradling